American Home

Wendell Garrett

David Larkin

Michael Webb

An Illustrated Documentary

American Home

From Colonial Simplicity
To The Modern Adventure

With essays by
James Howard Kunstler
Richard Guy Wilson
Denise Scott Brown

Photography by
Michael Freeman
and Paul Rocheleau

Universe

First published in the United States of America in 2001
by UNIVERSE PUBLISHING
A Division of Rizzoli International Publications, Inc.
300 Park Avenue South
New York, NY 10010

Designed by David Larkin

Universe Editor: Terence Maikels
Copy Editors: Lauren Wolfe, Bevin McLaughlin

Printed in China

Contents

Introduction

NOWHERE ELSE IN THE WORLD can compare with the variety of domestic architecture in America. While the earliest houses were largely derived from English prototypes, it was not long before structures evidenced intense regionalism, reflecting local tastes and vernacular and folk origins. The variety and dynamism in the style of homes in the emerging pluralistic society marches on today in homes designed by adventuresome architects and clients.

In the illustrated history of architecture the most attention has been paid to the grand buildings, the seats of authority, religion, and luxury. Less has been said about the house, its builders, craftsmen, and most importantly what it was like to live in, and how and why particular design features, furniture, furnishings, and artifacts came and went.

Over the past fifteen years, Paul Rocheleau, Michael Freeman, and I have travelled the continental United States making a visual record of historically typical and grand, homely and elegant, houses. In this visual documentary the pictures were taken to cover what one experiences in looking at a house—how it is seen from a distance and relates to the landscape, how a house is entered and the relative importance of all the rooms, how the building functioned, what life was like inside and outside, and how the furniture and fittings were used, bringing the experience of the historic American house back into life and providing a glimpse into domestic life in the next century.

The extraordinary story of the American house is first told through the styles on the New World landscape that originated in the British Isles, France, Germany, Italy, the Low Countries, Scandinavia, Eastern Europe, Spain, and North Africa. From the earliest period of simple New England timber-framing to a later period of elegant brick and stone, from Pennsylvania wedding chests to Chippendale chairs, architecture, interiors, workings, and the life experienced are explored.

In the nineteenth and early twentieth centuries the arriving cultures vastly expanded the variety of home building, from the log cabins and tiled stove-warmed interiors of the Scandinavians in the northern Midwest, to the Italian-American row house parlor and kitchen in the East. And the home builders were moving to the sunny West. The wide prairie invited the idea of single-level open-plan living, sparking the imagination of the young Frank Lloyd Wright and others. In the Southwest, the pine cabins of Anglo ranchers mingled with, then merged into, the more adaptable adobe houses sculpted for the earlier Spanish settlers. Further West, the new arrivals had by now an even wider variety of attitudes, cultures, plans and materials to employ. Which they certainly did, and enjoyed the bonus of decorative influences and simple proportions from China and Japan.

Today, for the most part, the center of creativity stays in the West and Southwest. No longer reliant on wood, brick and stone, the designers and their clients like their houses to bask in the sun, to evoke long shadows and provide cool interiors. There is something of an attempt at making sustainable homes by using solar power, but the driving motive is to make a statement of independence, even isolation, on the landscape. Here we will see the work of the adventurers, in dazzling variety, using their spaces to say what white columns and wrought iron gates said for their forebears. Given the increasing absence of the imaginative public client, that domestic landscape is the remaining area for untried talent, where the country's architectural design culture will survive.

Three distinguished essayists give their views on the American home as this documentary moves along. Richard Guy Wilson gives us the background to America's enduring love affair with the "Colonial" house. James Howard Kunstler spans the long period from the beginning of the nineteenth century that kicked off an incredible proliferation of ideas and borrowed styles, culminating in skillfully built and affordable centrally heated and electrically illuminated homes in the early twentieth century. Denise Scott Brown reminds us that from the end of World War II, just as with the colonial settlers' first homes, no architects are involved in most typical new houses. Unlike in the seventeenth century, there's scant thought for the future; creeping suburbia is put up by merchant builders. There are no real new towns but intense urbanism on the crust of emptying cities. The promise of designed prefabricated homes has faded into trailer parks and we are all ready for, at least, new regional strategies.

For the individual buildings illustrated here I am indebted to Wendell Garrett for most of the commentary up to the twentieth century and for Michael Webb from there onwards. They meet at Greene and Greene's Gamble House, where I invited both of their views.

Someone said to me once that all these beautifully photographed structures and interiors look a bit precious. They are.

DAVID LARKIN

Home and Colonial

Richard Guy Wilson

WHAT IS THE IMAGE that most Americans desire or envision for their place of residence? The question may seem trivial and irrelevant given the tremendous geographic and ethnic diversity that typifies the country, but the answer is quite easy: the Colonial or Early American style is far and away the favorite image for the American house.

Of course what can be identified as Early American or Colonial contains many dimensions and can be contentious. For many Americans, Colonial means the houses built along the eastern seaboard between the seventeenth and early nineteenth centuries, or between the various settlements at Jamestown, Plymouth, and Philadelphia, and the establishment of the United States as an independent country. Although 1776 is the date of Independence (or the declaration of) and 1783 is when the treaty with Britain was signed, most accounts of early American architecture include houses designed and built up to 1820 as part of the Colonial period, even though historically they might be called late Georgian, or Federal. But Colonial also means houses built under the Spaniards in Florida and the Southwest including California, by the French in Louisiana, Missouri, and Alabama, and the Dutch and Swedes in New York, New Jersey, and Delaware. "The Colonial Revival" is an umbrella term that gathers under it the many styles of Cape Cod saltbox, Georgian, James River plantation, Adamesque, Dutch, Spanish, Mission, Hacienda, Stockade, Raised Cottage, and even log cabin. Visit any town across the United States and you will immediately see the American fascination with the colonial past—it exists in banks, courthouses, and especially in residences. Even out on the far frontier of Montana and Washington, where white settlement did not begin until the second half of the nineteenth century, imitation Mount Vernons and New England clapboarded saltboxes appear.

Modern styles come and go, and most high-profile American modernists of the past century, from Frank Lloyd Wright to Frank Gehry, have sneered at this mania for Colonial reproductions. Yet when Americans list what they want a house to look like, the various forms of the Colonial dominate. Millions of people visit Colonial Williamsburg each year to step back into the eighteenth century. Yet much of Williamsburg is actually mid-twentieth century recreation of a mythic past that through its reproduction furniture, fabrics, paint colors, and model homes transformed and continues to influence how Americans live.

George Washington's Mount Vernon and Thomas Jefferson's Monticello are two of the most popular and visited of American homes; everybody knows them. Mount Vernon has inspired more American homes than any other building. Its long Potomac River portico and spindly columns reappear in a variety of guises from elegant country club estates with coupled paired columns, to split levels, with two-by-fours for support. With a two-story portico you are connected to history. In contrast, although Monticello graces the American nickel and is as well known, imitations appear much less frequently. Monticello is both too complex and too individual to serve as a housing model for most Americans.

The popularity of Colonial architecture results from many factors. On one level, these are the homes of the founding fathers and mothers, icons or relics of America's all-encompassing secular religion. The surviving houses are admired for their longevity; they have endured and stand as witnesses to earlier times. Their very materials—fieldstone in Pennsylvania, clapboard for New England, brick in Virginia, and adobe out West—exude the trials of their original builders and owners; they are romantic artifacts, nostalgic reminders of a mythic past. The size and scale of these houses helps contribute to the Colonial popularity. Although Colonial houses can range from very small to mansion-like in proportions, and they can dominate and swagger, a human scale is maintained. The houses are scaled to the individual and their ornament—the triangular pedimented doorway of the Sheldon Hawkes house in Deerfield, or the double porticos of Shirley in Virginia—are features of well-known faces. Certainly not every early American home is symmetrical; many variations exist, and the strung-out form with kitchen and service ells, and sometimes a barn, is part of the physiognomy of the period. And yet overall, balance seems to be a motif. The central prominent entrance, celebrating arrival and entry, and the entrance hall have become hallmarks of traditional American homes and continue today.

This nostalgic view of the beauty and attractiveness of Colonial American homes should have some balance with reality. What survives in most cases and are celebrated in this book, are the houses of the elite and the farmers. The standard house of the Colonial period was very simple, barely furnished, with a smoky fireplace. Most individuals shared beds, and classical details were rare. The economy that supported many of the larger houses both in the North and the South rested on slavery. Houses can represent many stories about their original owners and builders, and also the succeeding occupants who have lived in and preserved them over the years.

It is perhaps trite but true to say our homes are our castles; they are frequently a refuge and a metaphor for us, both personally and collectively. The Colonial house is the foundation stone of American architecture and of American values. From our houses spring many of our wishes, dreams, memories, and illusions. Our Colonial homes, both old and new, provide being, and well-being.

The First Shelters

In 1620, dissidents from the Anglican church embarked for the New World in a ship called the *Mayflower*. They stepped ashore at a place they named Plimouth.

More than half of the 101 passengers died in the first winter in New England. Life was harsh, and the need for food and shelter was predominant. By 1627, the Plimoth settlers had built a substantial village with dwellings, several common storehouses, shelters for livestock, and a meetinghouse. Today, Plimoth Plantation is a reconstructed village three miles from the original site that portrays the life of the Plimoth settlers in 1627. The buildings are based on evidence from written accounts, archaeological finds, and similar surviving buildings in England and the Low Countries dating from the same time. The village's furnishings are accurate reproductions of the kinds of things the settlers brought from England or made here.

The people who work in the village adopt the personalities and dress, and attempt the dialect of actual historical figures who lived at Plimoth. Life was centered on the street that divided the two rows of houses. In warm weather, it was a place to work and to meet. The small stockade-like redoubt near the center of this view was a constant reminder of the possible dangers of attack in the New World. The redoubt enclosed several small cannon whose range just reached the entrance gates, a last line of defense should an attack occur.

Many fences were necessary to prevent livestock from wandering into kitchen gardens or houses. The fences woven of sassafras saplings are very much like the wattle in the walls of buildings, to which the claylike daub was applied.

Also visible, at the left, are haystack-like piles of dried bundles of thatch, used for roofing. Other bundles of thatch just behind are drying against the wall.

Thirteen years earlier, in 1607, a less organized band of settlers landed in what came to be Jamestown, Virginia and stuggled to survive. Two years later only sixty of the original 214 were left. Supply ships came to keep alive the colony, which was enclosed within a fortified triangle of wooden palisaded walls.

Today there is a forty-year-old re-creation of the settlement. Inside the wooden stockade are structures representing Jamestown's earliest buildings, including homes, a church, and an armory. Interpreters are engaged in a variety of activities typical of daily life in the early seventeenth century, such as agriculture, animal care, and the preparation of meals. Most interesting is the architectural style, evoking the English late Middle Ages. The houses are all timber frame with wattle-and-daub walls and thatched roofs. The construction is of local timber, clay, and reeds. As weather and age take their toll, sections of the mud covering are allowed to fall away, with the constant repairs made as part of the interpretation.

A hearth corner at Plimoth shows an attempt to bring convenience and some comfort to a work space. The built-in settle, or bench, provides a place to sit; the window is placed where it can bring light into the work area. The whitewashed daub wall helps reflect what natural daylight enters through the door and small window.

The area is furnished typically for the period. On the shelf are a wooden platter, a whisk broom, and a ceramic butter pot. Hanging from a hook on the wall is an iron-and-brass skimmer. On the floor are a brass kettle, andirons, a simple stool, a lidded iron pot, and a wooden boxlike foot warmer, in which a ceramic dish could hold coals to bring warmth to the feet.

New England Begins

The houses were suited to the New England climate. The steep pitch of the roofs, a building tradition brought from the Old World, was well adapted to shed snow. Windows were small and few, to conserve heat. Open to the outside in warm weather, they were covered with oiled linen or paper in cold weather to keep out drafts but still bring in some light. At night and in the worst weather, interior shutters brought maximum warmth.

A well-furnished home at Plimoth shows fine furnishings brought from England. At the right is a court cupboard with stylish, elaborate turnings and carving. The room also has a carved and turned bed, hung with curtains for privacy and warmth; a mortar and pestle for grinding grain and other substances; and an earthenware chamber pot under the bed.

Meals in most Plimoth houses were prepared on the hearth in a smoke bay. In this simplest kind of arrangement, there was no chimney, simply a hole in the roof through which the smoke ascended. Inside, the hearth is separated from the rest of the house by a wattle-and-daub partition. A piece of woolen blanket hangs in front of the hearth at the top to keep smoke from coming into the room. The light coming through the boards at the back of the smoke bay comes from the through passage of this long house.

This hearth is typically furnished with such equipment as a twig broom, wooden water pail, iron pot with short legs to stand it in the embers, trammel to suspend the pot above the fire, chopping block for splitting kindling, iron poker, small green blown-glass bottle, wooden bowl, earthenware bowl, and stoneware drinking pot.

The hearth was the center of life in winter, when the family gathered around the fire to keep warm. In warm weather, sunlight from the open door helped bring light into this dark interior.

Puritan Simplicity

This corner of the Whipple House in Ipswich, Massachusetts, reflects the prosperity and taste of the owner. Early New England houses had frames of heavy hand-hewn timbers, usually oak, held together by mortise and tenon joints secured by wooden pegs.

In Essex County, Massachusetts, oak had become so scarce by 1660, because of the building boom, that the town of Ipswich was forced to issue felling rights to those who wanted to cut a white oak tree, with a ten-shilling penalty for every tree cut without permission. In their structural characteristics, these early New England houses show no variation from traditional English practices.

The oak frame was stiffened by angle braces at the corner posts and by heavy beams called chimney girts that ran completely across the house, abutting the chimney on either side.

From these chimney girts to the main girts on either side of the house ran another huge structural member, the summer beam. The story posts (sometimes called gunstock posts) are found at the front and rear of the building and support transverse summer beams. These intermediate story posts in the front and rear walls with a perceptible flare or jowl at the top may be referred to as wall posts, where they are only of one-story height.

It is probably to such a member that Increase Mather refers in his account of a bolt of lightning, in his Remarkable Providences, which struck a house in Marshfield, Plymouth Colony, in 1968, and "rent into shivers . . . one of the main posts of the house into which the summer [beam] was framed."

The Whipple House, was built around 1655 and before 1683, with later modifications. The first Massachusetts settlers were English, and these men and women never wholly ceased to be English. The seventeenth-century vernacular framed houses of Massachusetts Bay clearly enunciate the close relationship between the buildings the immigrants had grown up in and those they erected upon their arrival in the New World.

There were normally two entrances, front and back; as yet untainted by classicism, these doors were located well off center. A significant proportion of surviving seventeenth-century two-room, central-chimney houses at Massachusetts Bay commenced life as dwellings of single-room plan. Clearly, the immediate need for shelter under pioneer conditions, with no other housing available, as was the case in England, seems to have dictated for many of the settlers at every class or economic level a simple single-unit dwelling for a start, to be soon enlarged as their situation in life improved. Well-to-do John Whipple of Ipswich, a deputy to the General Court, apparently found the one-room plan a practical starting point.

America Takes Shape

The first houses of the Massachusetts Bay Colony were frequently left unpainted. The large central chimneys offered the best protection against the harsh New England winters.

The unprotected, weathered sheathing of the Sheldon-Hawks House is by far the most typical in appearance of early eighteenth-century structures in the mid-Connecticut River Valley. Settled in 1669, Deerfield, Massachusetts, was an exposed outpost in the wilderness for decades. In February 1704, Frenchmen led about 350 Indians in a dawn raid on the town. In five hours they killed forty-nine people and burned about half the town. They rounded up 112 prisoners and marched them 300 miles, in the dead of winter, to Canada. Twenty died on the way. Deerfield managed to survive and settlers returned in 1706.

This house was built by John Atkinson (1636–1702) on the upper green in Newbury, Massachusetts. It has been meticiously restored by his descendents. Early in the town's history the edges of the two greens, or commons, were divided into housing plots, and several historic structures still remain in place on them.

The John Alden House in Duxbury, Massachusetts, was built in 1653. The house, which stands on a knoll on the lot granted to Alden in 1627, is a weathered-shingle, two-story structure and was his second in Duxbury. A short distance away is the excavation of the cellar hole of the narrow house Alden built when he first moved to town.

The Mission House in Stockbridge, western Massachusetts, was begun in 1739 by the Reverend John Sergeant, but it was probably not completed until some years later. It is generally believed that the Mission House was constructed partly by Native Americans, eager to please Sergeant, and partly by Connecticut craftsmen, which may explain its distinctively Connecticut Valley front doorway. Sergeant's descendants continued to occupy the Mission House until 1867, when the property was sold.

Opposite, right.

The Rebecca Nurse homestead in Danvers, Massachusetts, was erected after the mid-seventeenth century and completed after 1700. The great hall of the Nurse homestead, seventeen by seventeen feet, was the original portion of the house, built on the single-room plan. The fireplace is seven feet wide, with two ovens inside. The walls were plastered white, and huge chamfered summer beams run from the front to the back of the house. The casement windows on both floors and in the garret were fitted with glass. Seventy-one-year-old Goodwife Nurse was condemned as a witch and died by hanging on July 19, 1692. The preservation of the homestead is her memorial, and on a stone monument near the John Greenleaf house Whittier has written her epitaph: "Oh Christian martyr who for truth could die when all about thee owned the hideous lie. The world redeemed from superstition's sway is breathing freer for thy sake today." Without exception the earliest surviving framed houses of one-room plan at Massachusetts Bay have been added to, most of them enlarged not once but several times. The first extension was normally in a longitudinal direction; the first colonists were surely familiar with this contemporary English concept. The main stairs then occupy a location opposite the front entrance in front of the chimney. The typical solution for service rooms (buttery, pantry, and dairy), particularly as the century wore on, was a lean-to extending the entire length of the house at the rear, divided into three distinct areas. By the later decades of the seventeenth century, the "saltbox" profile seems to have become relatively standard at Massachusetts Bay.

The kitchen of the Wells-Thorn House in Deerfield, Massachusetts, was built about 1717. The original portion of the house was probably built after Ebenezer Wells, a farmer and tavern keeper in Deerfield, bought the property in 1717. The traditional heavy framing must have given comfort to frontier settlers living in constant fear of Indian attacks and violent storms. The feather-edged vertical sheathing boards were milled at a time when virgin forests still yielded tall pines exceeding the legal limit of twenty-four inches in diameter. The massive hearth of the kitchen is remarkably bare, and has been furnished with only the items that were common in this area around 1725, according to information found in household inventories. The equipment around the hearth includes a peel, used to place and remove loaves, pies, and other baked goods from the oven; a lugpole, from which to suspend pots and kettles; tongs, to move embers; a brass kettle; three iron hooks; a "knife and flesh fork," or long-handled, two-pronged fork; a "spider," or skillet on legs; and a bell metal (an alloy of copper and tin) skillet, the single most expensive piece here when it was new. On the floor are two sacks of grain, a hoe, and an ax.

Below is the pantry off the kitchen. As in the seventeenth century, a warm lean-to kitchen on the first-floor level generally had two adjacent service rooms: One was a cool all-purpose "pantry" directly off the kitchen, used fundamentally for the storage of pots, pans, and eating utensils, and certain foodstuffs as well, including those requiring lower temperatures; the other was the "buttery," used for drink and dairy products. The pantry exemplifies the old New England adage: "A place for everything and everything in its place." The contents of the Wells-Thorn House pantry are an accurate representation of the numbers and types of things stored in Connecticut River Valley pantries around 1725, as gleaned from probate inventories. The contents include (from top to bottom) a pewter dish; dark-green blown-glass bottles; a pewter basin; "treen," or turned wooden bowls and plates; and a sieve.

Wood, Brick, and Stone

Most clapboard houses were not painted at all until after 1800. This was because paint was costly. Even so, it was more affordable than the most sophisticated forms of decoration inside or out, such as carved stone, wallpaper, or other expensive luxuries.

This house, built in 1752 by Joseph Webb of Wethersfield, Connecticut, shows the vivid colors that style-conscious home owners favored at that time. Scraping away the layers of paint to find the bottom layer and using scientific analysis revealed the bright red, blue, and yellow that have been matched in restoration.

All through the Colonial period and until well after the Revolution, new villages were settled throughout New England. Through the years the roof pitch grew less steep than it was at first; the chimney became square rather than high and narrow; ceilings were plastered over; walls were paneled; the house was sometimes painted; and swinging casement windows gave way to up and down sash. We call this new style or fashion Georgian after the line of English kings who came to the throne in 1714. It was formal and showy rather than functional and picturesque; it was symmetrical in design; it looked to the rules of ancient classical architecture and insisted that the frame now be fully dressed in a wooden casing. These fine Georgian country houses still had the traditional oblong form but more nearly approached a square in plan, with four full-sized rooms to a floor and two full stories, front and back. Above all, the front door gave the impression of a miniature classical temple with pediment and flat pilasters. Not until the beginning of the eighteenth century, when settlements were well established and a lively commerce began to bring in new wealth, did the colonists find the leisure and means to give their architectural tastes freer reign. In the country, village builder and squire alike depended upon the English architectural pattern books, called builder's guides, to help them design and build a house in the "new taste."

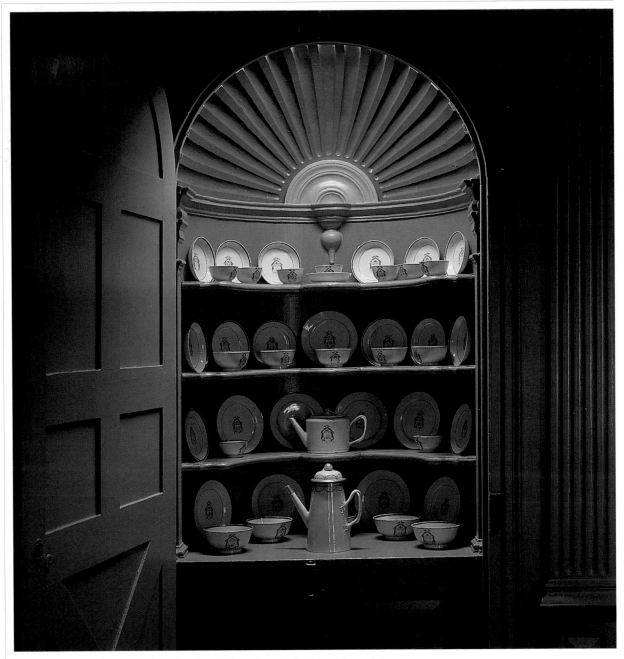

The handsomely carved and colorfully painted shell cupboard in the Joseph Webb House in Wethersfield, Connecticut, must have been one of the most pleasing parts of the house for the Webb family. It is built into the left side of the fireplace wall; on the right side is a passage to the room beyond. The cupboard has been repainted based on paint analysis by the Society for the Preservation of New England Antiquities. Here is displayed a set of Chinese export porcelain, decorated to order with a family crest. Given the design, Chinese artisans hand-painted each piece to match. The set includes a teapot (center) and a taller coffeepot (directly below). The cupboard below probably stored larger pieces of the set, such as tureens and platters.

25

The kitchen in the Mission House contains the largest of the four fireplaces in the house. On display are American culinary and domestic utensils of the eighteenth and nineteenth centuries and, above the mantel, a French musket of the mid-eighteenth century.

The pine paneling in the parlor of the Mission House is stained to resemble walnut. The cupboard contains English and Dutch earthenware, most dating from the 1660s to the 1760s. That the house was grand for its time may be judged by the fact that when John Sergeant died prematurely of a fever in 1749, he owed more than seven hundred pounds for expenses incurred while building his house.

Above The keeping room or second parlor of the Ashley House, Sheffield, Massachusetts.

Left The buttery or "storeroom for provisions" of the Ashley House. The number of potters who were plying their trade in New England at an early date is astonishing: at least three hundred were at work before 1800. These men used the common clay that was abundant along the beds of streams—the kind familiar to us in house bricks. Their earliest ware was called "redware," or sometimes "brownware," an indication of the color of the body after firing. In the eighteenth century, potters supplied the baking dishes and storage pots for the household and, to a considerable extent, smaller forms that supplemented pewter and woodenware on the table. Many jars, pitchers, and bowls were glazed both on the outside and the inside, but other utililitarian forms were glazed on the interior surface only. Certain objects, such as milk pans and the common pot—an all-purpose vessel of cylindrical shape rounded in a bit at the bottom—looked almost the same, for as long as the craft survived.

The General Sylvanus Thayer Birthplace in Braintree, Massachusetts, was built in 1720. It was originally built in the country in the clapboard style of earlier Colonial houses, not as a stylish house with the most up-to-date features, and the lean-to was added about 1755. The lean-to housed a kitchen (heretofore cooking had been done in the hall), a keeping room, and a pantry. About the time the lean-to was added, twelve-over-twelve windows were hung in the front of the house, replacing the original leaded casements, and the thrifty Yankees hung the old casements in the lean-to at the back. Lean-tos, either added or original to the house, are common in New England, and houses with the characteristic short roof pitch in front and a long pitch sweeping close to the ground in back are called "saltboxes."

Made of massive hand-hewn oak timbers, the house frame served as a large skeleton for support of the enclosing walls and roof. The framing timbers were of a huge size because they had to carry a heavy load of clay or brick nogging within the walls. Most of the joints in a Colonial frame are varieties of the mortise-and-tenon, cut into the timbers with auger, chisel, and mallet. The tenon, or flange, fits into the mortise, or socket; a hole is bored through the whole joint and a round wooden pin, known as a treenail (pronounced "trunnel"), runs through the joint to secure it. The exterior wall surface was almost invariably made of clapboards. The studs were vertical timbers, spaced about two feet on centers, and framed into the sill below and the girt above.

The large kitchen in the lean-to was added to the Thayer birthplace about 1755, with a large selection of kitchenwares. The architectural and domestic focus of a Colonial home was the great fireplace. As with the chimney stack, it was made of fieldstone or of brick. The fireplace was considerably larger than that of today for two reasons: The fireplace was a heating unit, and a fire of big hardwood logs was kept burning all the time in cold weather. It was also a cooking unit, and because of large families and the relatively large amount of meat consumed, needed to have plenty of room for roasting spits, stewpots, and the like.

The "mantel tree" or lintel across the fireplace opening was sometimes of stone, but in the biggest fireplaces, such as in this house, was a squared timber of oak as much as ten by eighteen inches in section. Its height above the hearth was sufficient to keep it from burning, though it often became charred. The equipment of the earliest fireplaces consisted of a green wood lug pole bisecting the chimney flue six or eight feet above the hearth; from it hung the pot chains and "trammels" (pot hooks of adjustable length). When iron was available, an iron rod, usually lower, took the place of a wooden trammel bar. Later, the familiar swinging iron crane, fastened by eyes set into the masonry at one side, served as a support for hooks and trammels—an obvious improvement as the pots could now swing away from the blaze for inspection during cooking. The earliest supports for the logs were simple iron dogs; the more graceful and elaborate andirons of wrought iron or polished brass are generally of eighteenth-century date.

The dining room in Clifford S. Bonney's House in Newbury, Massachusetts, with late seventeenth- and eighteenth-century furnishings. A general pattern of establishing a town began to emerge in Massachusetts Bay within a decade after 1630. First a group of settlers, usually numbering thirty or forty adult males, petitioned the General Court for a grant of land for the purpose of founding a new community. An exploratory committee for the new group looked for an unoccupied region well endowed with natural meadowland, ample water, good woodland, and accessibility to the more settled parts of the colony. A land committee chose a suitable location for the village center, if possible on a site that could be easily defended against Native Americans—perhaps alongside a river, as in the case of Newbury. The quest for farmland and cattle raising brought the first settlers to Newbury. The town, established in 1635, soon developed several distinct areas of settlement. One was the original town site along the banks of the Parker River; another was "the waterside," a few miles to the north along the southern edge of the Merrimack. Old-towners were almost exclusively farmers harvesting the salt hay of the marshes and raising cattle. But the waterside people had chosen an ideal site for a seaport. The gently sloping bank provided a firm foundation for shipbuilding with the timber of the hinterland; the broad mouth of the Merrimack protected by Plum Island formed a safe harbor. Newburyport—unlike Newbury, its agrarian parent—would derive vitality, wealth, and glamour from the sea.

30

The Old Manse in Concord, Massachusetts, built as his parsonage by the Reverend William Emerson in 1769 or 1770, and looks much as it did when it was new, except for the gabled window built into the roof by the Reverend Samuel Ripley in 1845. The Old Manse is rich in literary associations. Nathaniel Hawthorne and his wife, Sophia, rented the house for three years from the heirs of Ripley, who had lived in it after his marriage to the Reverend Emerson's widow until he died in 1841. The first night they spent there was their wedding night, July 9, 1842, and the Hawthornes' life at the Manse lasted until October 1845. During this period he wrote a number of stories that were later gathered in Mosses from an Old Manse and the second edition of Twice-Told Tales and were sold to magazines. On March 3, 1844, the Hawthorne's first child, Una, was born in the upstairs bedroom. "It was worthy to have been one of the time-honored parsonages of England in which, through many generations, a succession of holy occupants pass from youth to age, and bequeath each an inheritance of sanctity to pervade the house and hover over it as with an atmosphere," runs Hawthorne's description of his home in Mosses. "It was awful," he added, "to reflect how many sermons must have been written there." When the Hawthornes left the house, they returned to Salem where he took a job at the Custom House.

The wallpaper in the front hall of the Old Manse in Concord, Massachusetts, is a reproduction of a French trompe l'oeil paper of about 1780, which became very popular in America. A sample of the original paper is preserved under glass in the upstairs hall. Above the table hangs a portrait of Daniel Bliss Ripley, the youngest son of Ezra and Phebe Bliss Emerson Ripley. The door from the hall opens into the large parlor.

Concord is doubly famed: as the site of the second engagement of the Revolution at Old North bridge (the site of "the shot heard round the world") and as the home of the great literary flowering in the first half of the nineteenth century. Three giants of American literature—Ralph Waldo Emerson, Nathaniel Hawthorne, and Henry David Thoreau—lived and wrote in Concord. Emerson lived in the Old Manse in 1834 and 1835 and wrote his first book, Nature, in a second-floor study. Nature, in the words of the historian Samuel Eliot Morison, "may be taken as opening a period in American literary culture corresponding to 1775 in American politics." The old house and its grounds were the setting that gave Hawthorne's imagination a frame for its inter-weaving of present reality with a mythical past. In his three years at the Manse, Hawthorne was living out, and turning into litera-ture a Yankee pastoral that would do for New England what Washington Irving's "Legend of Sleepy Hollow" had done for New York. In years to come—after Salem and The Scarlet Letter, after Lenox and The House of the Seven Gables, after Europe and a consulate's position—the Hawthornes would return to Concord and buy a house.

The Quaker Influence

The two-story section of the house of John Bartram's Garden in Philadelphia, Pennsylvania, comprises the original Swedish farmhouse, which had a gambrel roof. When Bartram built the east façade in 1770, he extended the other side of the house by the depth of one room. The one-story addition at the right and a corresponding one at the opposite end of the building were added in the 1820s by Ann Bartram Carr, his granddaughter, who installed the dormers at the same time. The Quaker John Bartram, the first America-born botanist, began acquiring land on the lower Schuylkill River in 1728 with an initial purchase of 112 acres, to which he gradually added. Here he created a world-renowned farm and garden.

Most of the land he farmed, but a few acres near the house he terraced for the cultivation of North American plants, many of which he gathered on collecting trips that ranged as far afield as Florida. Within a few years the elder Bartram had a brisk trade in shipping roots and seeds to wealthy Englishmen. So great had his fame become by 1765 that George III appointed him Royal Botanist with an annual stipend of £50 (which continued until the outbreak of the Revolution). Linnaeus called him "the greatest natural botanist in the world." His son, William Bartram, continued his father's explorations in the Carolinas, Georgia, and Florida and with his brother operated the garden and nursery, shipping roots and seeds throughout the United States and Europe. Gradually they added greenhouses and increased their sale of live plants, which could be ordered from the catalogues they produced.

Above is a view of Bartram's study at historic Bartram's Garden. John Bartram's early interest in plants was encouraged probably by James Logan. In 1728 he laid out a botanic garden on land he bought at Kingsessing on the Schuylkill and began what were most likely the first hybridizing experiments in America. He began a correspondence and exchange of specimens with Peter Collinson, the English plantsman, in 1733; through Collinson, Bartram's American plants were distributed abroad and he became internationally celebrated. In 1765, as Royal Botanist, he journeyed from Charleston, South Carolina, to St. Augustine, Florida, and explored the St. John's River by canoe; on this trip he observed all forms of life, examined mineral resources, and prepared a map of the river. Bartram's ideas anticipated modern thinking, particularly in geology. As a freethinker who was expelled from his Quaker meeting for denying the divinity of Christ, he had these words carved in a second-floor stone panel: "It is God alone Almyty Lord / The Holy One by he adored / John Bartram 1770." His suggestion of a great survey trip westward, made to Benjamin Franklin, bears a strong resemblance to Jefferson's later instructions to Lewis and Clark.

In the bedchamber in John Bartram's house, located directly over the parlor downstairs; some family estate inventories have survived to guide the refurnishing. Above the fireplaces throughout the house are handsome paneled chimney breasts containing small cupboards. They and the rest of the woodwork are painted to resemble the original colors as determined by paint analysis. The elder Bartram died in September 1777, three days after the battle of Brandywine Creek, very much worried that the British might destroy his "darling garden." However, General Sir William Howe saw to it that no harm came to the garden even though British officers camped on the property. Bartam left the part of his estate that included his house and botanical garden to his son John Jr., who shared his father's interest in horticulture. His other son, William, the renowned naturalist and a bachelor, lived for the rest of his life with his brother and his family following a four-year expedition to the deep South. Between 1773 and 1777 the younger Bartram traveled, lived among the Indians, collected plants, noted his observations, and sketched. *His Travels Through North and South Carolina, Georgia, East and West Florida, the Cherokee Country, etc.*, is the chief cause of his fame, a literary as well as a scientific triumph.

The southeast corner of Wright's Ferry Mansion. The placement of the elongated windows with small panes opposite each other on both sides of the house, the pent cove between the first and second stories, and the cove cornice are all characteristic of the early Georgian style as interpreted by English Quakers in Pennsylvania. The long, narrow plan of the house is also typically English and was common in early Pennsylvania houses. Despite the predominance of such English characteristics, the side-lapped shingles, among other elements, are indicative of the local German workmen who undoubtedly helped construct the house. The English Quaker heritage so strongly evident in the architecture of the house and its furnishings, and the remarkable character of its original owner and her important ties with Philadelphia, make Wright's Ferry Mansion an important embodiment of early eighteenth-century America.

The west façade of Wright's Ferry Mansion, Columbia, Pennsylvania, which was built in 1738 for Susanna Wright. It was the house she lived in from 1738, when it was built, until 1756 or 1757. Susanna Wright and her family came to Pennsylvania from Lancashire, England, and settled initially in Chester, just outside Philadelphia. Within a few years, she was corresponding with James Logan, William Penn's secretary and one of the most influential public figures in Pennsylvania during the first half of the eighteenth century. An astute politician, fur merchant, linguist, scientist, and bibliophile, Logan encouraged Susanna to study languages and literature, sending her books from his own extensive library. These delighted her intellect and prompted her to do a great deal of writing, samples of which she would send to Logan. In 1726, about the time Logan was making plans to build his own country mansion, Stenton, in Germantown, Susanna Wright purchased a hundred acres at a remote spot on the east bank of the Susquehanna River. The Wrights were among several prominent English Quaker families to settle in this distant part of western Chester County. James Logan also owned land here. He probably encouraged its settlement because of its potential importance in stabilizing a territory that was claimed by both Pennsylvania and Maryland due to an inaccuracy in the original charter. Moreover, it was an area threatened by uncertain relations with Native Americans.

The entrance hall of Wright's Ferry Mansion evokes seventeenth-century design with its brick floor, massive Dutch doors at each end, and magnificent staircase with turned balusters. The vitality of those turnings is repeated in the stretcher-base and gateleg tables and wainscot chair, all of which were made in Philadelphia of walnut. The turned chair is a rare surviving example of the Philadelphia interpretation of the Cromwellian chair that was popular in England and the New England colonies.

Opening up this region was important for secure westward expansion. In 1730, with Logan's assistance, the Wrights obtained a patent for a road from the ferry to the town of Lancaster. Lancaster was the seat of Lancaster County, which had been set off from Chester County in 1729. As the Wrights had been instrumental in establishing the new county, it was named in honor of their native Lancashire, England.

The early Georgian character of the parlor of Wright's Ferry Mansion is apparent in the architectural paneling. The arched doors with their keystones are somewhat less sophisticated than those in Philadelphia houses. In accord with inventories of Quaker households from the same region and period, the floors and windows have been left bare and the rooms are sparsely furnished. This shows the elegant simplicity of design popular among English Quakers, who, in the first half of the eighteenth century, dominated Pennsylvania culturally as well as politically.

The quality of the furnishings reflects the fact that the Wrights knew and patronized the same fine Philadelphia cabinetmakers used by their friends, who were among the most affluent individuals in that city. Although Philadelphia would have been Susanna Wright's primary source for furnishings, she undoubtedly also patronized local, Germanic sources for purely utilitarian pieces.

Oven at the back of the summer kitchen in the ell off the back of the Peter Wentz Farmstead. Baking in these beehive-shaped ovens relied on a combination of radiation from the walls and, to a lesser extent, air convection to heat the food. As new settlers crossed the Atlantic and arrived in America, they introduced their own traditional dishes, adapting them to suit the materials available. The English contributed apple pie; the Dutch, cookies (koekjes), coleslaw (kool: cabbage, and sla: salad), and waffles; the Germans, sauerkraut; and the Pennsylvania Germans scrapple. American victuals became in time a mirror of history, the names of the country's dishes reflecting the medley of its peoples, religions, places, and even occupations. There was Shaker loaf, burgoo, Maryland chicken, snickerdoodles, spoon bread, cowpoke beans, hush puppies, jambalaya, pandowdy, Boston-baked beans, Philadelphia pepper pot, Moravian sugar cake, Swedish meatballs, haymaker's switchel, and whaler's toddy. In 1796, Amelia Simmons published American Cookery, the first cookbook to be published in America and the first to contain Native American specialties. Simmons included in her forty-seven-page compendium such dishes as Indian slapjack (pancakes), johnnycake, pickled watermelon rind, "cramberry" sauce, Jerusalem artichokes, spruce beer, Indian pudding, "pumpkin" pie, a gingerbread that is much softer than the thin European variety, and six kinds of rice pudding.

The Peter Wentz Farmstead in Worcester, Pennsylvania, constructed in 1758 by American-born Peter Wentz Jr., on land purchased by his German emigrant father in 1743. The two-and-one-half-story, five-bay, double-pile stone house, with pent eaves between the stories and balcony, probably stood out in the eighteenth century as one of the larger dwellings in what now is Worcester Township, Montgomery County. While the west front is built of dressed stone, the other walls (seen here) are rubble stone. The house shares much with Anglo-Welsh stone houses of the time, there are also appealing Germanic grace notes such as the German-language house blessing, the extensive use of five-plate stoves, and the painted decoration. That George Washington twice had his headquarters at the farmstead gives it an historic importance equal to its architectural importance. Following his failure to check the British advance on Philadelphia at Brandywine Creek, in September 1777, Washington withdrew his army across the Schuykill, which had the advantage of putting his army on the Philadelphia side of the river. Once he had determined to attack, he moved down Skippack Pike, pausing at Peter Wentz's house before striking southeast into the heart of Germantown, where the colonists hoped to surprise the British on October 4. Following the collapse of that attack, the colonial army retired back to Skippack Creek, and Washington returned to the Wentz house. He was there when news came of Burgoyne's surrender at Saratoga—an event that proved to be the turning point in the American Revolution.

Spotted decoration was applied all over the walls of the winter kitchen of the Peter Wentz Farmstead. The restoration of the mid-eighteenth-century house revealed that the original interior colors—yellow, salmon, and blue—differed from those thought at the time to be typical in Pennsylvania Colonial houses. More dramatically, the restoration team determined that these colors had been applied in sponged decorative patterns of boldly applied dots, stripes, and commas. Appropriate to the time and place, and confirmed by the Wentz and similar household inventories, there are no curtains at the windows and no carpets on the floor. Colors have been recreated in the rooms from a microscopic chemical examination of the original surfaces.

German immigrants started to arrive in Philadelphia in 1683, owing in large part to William Penn's promise of religious toleration. On Penn's second visit to America, he established a unicameral legislature and guaranteed freedom of worship to those believing in "One almighty God," under the democratic Charter of Privileges that would remain Pennsylvania's form of government until the American Revolution. The colony's official policy of religious toleration brought many Germans, whose hard work and farming skills made Pennsylvania an exporter of food to other colonies.

The Pitt-Dixon House in Williamsburg, Virginia is a reconstruction of the house built by George Pitt between 1717 and 1719. His apothecary shop, the Sign of the Rhinoceros, stood behind the house. In 1774 Pitt sold the house to John Dixon, who published the Virginia Gazette in the building next door. The original Pitt-Dixon house was destroyed by fire in 1896, but was rebuilt in 1936. The domestic architecture in Williamsburg was a marriage between substance and style. It joined English forms and traditions with native materials like "heart" pine, superbly straight-grained and everlasting wood cut from the center of trees that had grown slowly for centuries in the Tidewater's dense forests. It suited not only Virginia's climate, with high-ceilinged rooms and one-room-deep plans that fostered ventilation, but also the social lives and mores of its new client-inhabitants. As Hugh Jones wrote in The Present State of Virginia (1724): "Here . . . they build with brick, but most commonly with timber. . . . Thus their houses are lasting, dry, and warm in winter, and cool in summer; especially if there be windows enough to draw the air. Thus they dwell comfortably, genteelly, pleasantly, and plentifully in this delightful, healthful, and (I hope) thriving city of Williamsburg."

Opposite, right

The maple armchair in the left foreground of the seventeenth-century room in the Pitt-Dixon House, made in New England about 1660, is drawn up to a late-seventeenth-century English double-gateleg table covered with Alpujarra carpet. The late-seventeenth-century brass chandelier hanging over the table is Dutch or English. Beside the fireplace is an English stump work writing coffer on a New York dropleaf trestle-base table, made in about 1700. Over the mantel a breastplate and matching back piece from a suit of armor, attributed to a Milanese armoror of about 1575, are mounted on either side of an Italian cabasset of the same period. The white-oak-and-pine chest of drawers between the windows, made in eastern Massachusetts about 1690, retains traces of its original red paint. Beside the chest is an English beechwood chair of about 1690. The English traveler Hugh Jones wrote 25 years after Williamsburg's founding: "They live in the same neat manner, dress after the same modes, and behave themselves exactly as the gentry in London. . . . The habits, life, customs, computations, &c. of the Virginians are much the same as about London, which they esteem their home."

The maple-and-chestnut table with turned stretchers against the wall in the parlor of the Pitt-Dixon House was probably made in Massachusetts about 1700. The tabletop is inset with slate cut to conform to its octagonal shape. Behind the tea table is a walnut Spanish-foot easy chair made in Boston about 1710, and between the windows stands a black-walnut dressing table, probably made in Philadelphia about 1710; its curved, crossed stretchers and arched skirt make it a fine early example of the form. The late-seventeenth-century looking glass above it is also from Philadelphia. Another early Pennsylvania piece is the walnut desk in the corner, which was made about 1720. The overmantel portrait of William Ashe is attributed to Sir Peter Lely. The itinerant clergyman Andrew Burnaby visited Williamsburg in the late 1750s and noted: "Although the houses are of wood, covered with shingles . . . the whole makes a handsome appearance. . . . Upon the whole, it is an agreeable residence . . . and at the times of the assemblies, and general courts, it is crowded with the gentry of the country: on those occasions there are balls and other amusements; but as soon as the business is finished, they return to their plantations; and town is in a manner deserted."

Communal Living

In the eighteenth century the New World continued to offer refuge and the hope of peace for pious and hardworking religious groups from parts of fractious and intolerant Europe. Among the first were Protestants from Moravia who settled in the Carolina upcountry, and semi-monastic German Baptists who founded the austere cloistered Ephrata colony near Lancaster in Pennsylvania, but brought with them a tradition of music and fine printing. Later, the Shakers arrived led by the zealous Ann Lee, seeking separation from the rest of the world and celibacy for both sexes. Yet they, more than any utopian group, have given us a legacy of equality, tolerance, common sense, and wonderful spare design.

Above

A view of the Shaker Church Family village in Hancock, Massachusetts. Showing, from left to right, the Laundry and Machine Shop, built in the 1790s; Dwelling, 1830–31; Sisters' Dairy and Weave Shop, about 1795–1820; small brick Ministry Wash House, mid-nineteenth century; Poultry House, 1878; and Round Stone Barn, 1826–64. The religious principle of separation from the world led to the society's quest for economic self-sufficiency. The Shakers attempted to establish their villages on a sound financial basis. Hundreds of acres of land were signed over to the society by converts, and the Believers purchased additional tracts with community resources. Farmlands were cleared, woodlots logged, orchards planted, and gardens cultivated. The society built mills for grinding its own flour and sawing lumber, which subsequently became a source of income from non-Shaker neighbors. The Believers constructed barns and sheds for storing crops and feed and housing animals. They built shops and offices, dwellings and meeting houses. They planted cash crops and "manufactured" marketable items to be sold to the "world"; with that income they purchased the goods they could not produce on their own. The buildings constructed by the Shakers may be among their most lasting endeavors. Every village could point with pride to at least one edifice—at Hancock Shaker Village, the Church Family round stone barn built by Daniel Goodrich in 1826 drew the most attention. Ingenious in design with many practical advantages, it stands as an exception to the Shakers' preference for linear living space. The round stone barn required enormous resources and commitment to complete.

Opposite

The workshop and residence was built by Church Family Shakers at Sabbathday Lake, Maine, in 1839, for two women and two men in the Maine Ministry. Two female leaders occupied the second floor, over the male leaders on the first floor. In 1875, the Church Family enlarged and improved this Ministry Shop and Residence. The large two-over-two windowpanes replaced the earlier windows in 1910. The physical arrangement of Shaker villages followed no single plan. Yet in most cases the meetinghouse bulked large on the mental landscape, for it was the dwelling of the ministry and the central site for religious gatherings. Likewise, the office assumed prominence because it was where the trustees lived and carried out the business transactions of the world. Neither, however, was the physical center of life for an ordinary Believer. The family dwelling was the focal point of an individual's existence and the primary focus of daily activities. The dwelling, whether a large dormitory specially designed for the Believers or a smaller building adapted to their needs, was the hub of a complex of buildings and outbuildings, including shops, mills, barns, and washhouses as well as sheds, pens, and stables and surrounding dooryards, gardens, fields, woodlots, walkways, and fences.

Ephrata Cloister, near Lancaster, Pennsylvania, was a religious commune founded in 1732 by Conrad Beissel, a mystic who had come to Germantown, Pennsylvania, from his native Germany twelve years before. "Ephrata," the Hebrew word for plentiful, was an early name for Bethlehem. Ephrata Cloister members lived a monastic life of work and religious devotion, according to the tenets of German pietists who had influenced Beissel when he was a young man. The emphasis in the Cloister was on mystical revelation and brotherhood rather than on ritual and creed.

The faithful celebrated the Sabbath on Saturday, as Jews do, and on occasion they observed communion and the early-Christian practice of washing the feet as a symbolic act of humility. The cloister faithful constructed their buildings in the styles of their native Rhineland. Mostly built between 1735 and 1750, they have been restored to their original appearance and furnished to illustrate the way of life of their original occupants.

Ephrata was neither the first nor the largest utopian community in antebellum America, but it was among the most durable of the pietistic groups. By the middle of the eighteenth century its numbers may have reached three hundred; in 1900 there were seventeen remaining brethren and sisters. Ephratans, and most pietists, never intended to proselytize. Spiritual contemplation was the essence of Ephrata; for the faithful, heaven on earth was not a distant hope but an immediate expectation. These earnest utopians had great confidence in their way of life. Detaching themselves from worldly society, freed of its imperfections, they believed they would create an ideal social system made up of truly moral men and women.

Each of the three floors of the Sisters' House at Ephrata Cloister had a separate kitchen, where food for the sisters living on that floor was prepared. The stone sink between the windows has a drain that leads through the log wall to the outside. The eighteenth-century poplar table was made at the cloister and stands on a copy of the original lime-mortar floor. The Ephrata Society consisted of three orders: a celibate sisterhood, a celibate brotherhood, and a married order of householders. Dressed in long, white, hooded habits, the celibates toiled twelve hours a day farming and growing fruit on some two hundred acres of land. They also ran grist, paper, saw, fulling, and oil mills and a print shop and bindery. The sisters were responsible for baking, making cloth, and cooking the one meager vegetarian meal that the celibates were allowed each day. The Ephrata Society persisted until the last celibate sister died in 1813. The married householder members then continued the congregation until 1934 under the name of the German Seventh Day Baptist Church.

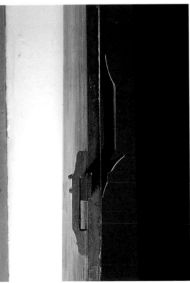

Detail of an interior door in the Ephrata Brothers' House, built about 1746. The door is made from a single tulip-poplar board, which measures 67 by 22.5 inches. The wooden hinges are dovetailed into wooden battens that in turn are dovetailed into the door.

Wooden latches of this design are found throughout the buildings at Ephrata. Economy and the availability of woodworkers among the brothers probably dictated the extensive use of wooden hardware.

In 1753, a small group of Moravians left Pennsylvania to establish a settlement in North Carolina called Bethabara. Like the settlers at Plimoth more than a century earlier, the Moravians came to the New World for the sake of religious freedom. Their first task was to clear the land and build homes. By 1765, the Moravians had so prospered that plans were made for a fine new town, to be called Salem. By 1772, the new town was ready for occupancy.

The Moravians were a religious group originating in Europe as followers of Jan Hus, a Bohemian who was one of the first Protestant martyrs in the early fifteenth century. The spirit of the Moravian way of life is captured in the phrase: "In essentials, unity; in nonessentials, liberty; in all things, charity."

The early Moravians were semicommunal and divided themselves into different groups or choirs: Married People, Single Sisters, Single Brothers, Widows, Widowers, Older Girls, Older Boys, and Children. Single adults shared communal houses, one for each gender. Everybody, however, sought to live and share peaceably, as members of a single, large, and devout family.

Here, long tables—one an original, the rest copies—in a common dining room point to the communal nature of Moravian life. Communal dining rooms were used by Single Brothers and Single Sisters; other members of the community dined in family units.

The kitchen in the Church Family Dwelling was built at Hancock Shaker Village from 1830 to 1831 and was designed to feed a communal family of nearly a hundred people with efficiency. A rotating team of "kitchen Sisters" worked with state-of-the-art equipment in a room that was characteristically light, airy, and located on the basement level. The two ovens with built-in arch kettles were used for steaming, boiling, and stewing large quantities of food. In contrast to their neighbors in "the World," who still stooped over hearths to cook (until the cast-iron cookstove became more common by the 1850s), Shaker women worked at convenient, comfortable waist height. The floor was designed for both the safety and comfort of the women who worked here, combining fireproof marble near the wood-fired equipment, with wooden floors, easier on the legs, in the work areas. The oven on the left was designed by Count Rumford in the 1820s; behind the iron door are narrow shelves for baking pies. The lead builder and designer, Elder William Deming, was proud of the new accommodations: "The cook room is very convenient; we have excellent water from a never failing spring that is conveyed into the cook room in three different places and two places in the second loft. There are two excellent ovens made on an improved plan which will bake four different settings at one heating. Also the arch kettles are on a new plan of my own invention, and which proves to be the best ever seen about here."

In the dining room, in the Church Family Dwelling at Hancock Shaker Village, Sisters and Brothers ate meals together but sat on opposite sides of the communal dining room. They dined in silence for practical as well as spiritual reasons—the chatter of nearly a hundred voices is deafening in a room of plain plaster walls and pine floors. Windows on the inner wall to the left admitted daylight into the stairwells to the kitchen below. The large transom over the doors carried light into the first-floor hall. The food of the Shakers varied from village to village. Believers were to be content with the "common" diet, not indulging their appetites or asking for special provisions unless illness required it. The kitchen was declared the province of the cooks and normally off-limits to other family members. These regulations were designed to maintain order and to curb natural impulses. Specific orders prohibited eating raw or unripe fruit and nuts, cucumbers without salt or pepper, and freshly baked bread. The society's dietary ordinances in the early decades of the nineteenth century did not extend beyond these few constraints. As a result, the food that was served reflected local supplies and regional preferences. Seafood, for example, was a special treat in the eastern villages, but not among the Kentucky Shakers, where southern cuisine was more common. Menus fluctuated with the season and with the capacity of the families to preserve and store foodstuffs. Fresh vegetables and fruits made the summer and autumn fare more nutritious and varied for Believers and non-Shakers alike. In general, the members of Shaker society ate well.

47

Above are the dining room doors in the Church Family Dwelling at Hancock Shaker Village. The official rules of the society mandated high standards of communal cleanliness and neatness. The interiors and exteriors of buildings were to be kept orderly and in good repair. The dwelling house was filled with chairs and tables, beds and bureaus, stoves and woodboxes, lamps and chests, tools and utensils, foodstuffs, and other supplies. The social space that remained was congested, if not crowded, with people and allowed little room for privacy. Such peculiar features of Shaker architecture as double entrances, double doors, and parallel staircases did little to reduce the general congestion in the dwelling; others, including the large number of peg rails and built-in chests of drawers, were more helpful. Group activities took place in the larger confines of the dining area and the family meeting room. The dooryard, which served as an extension of the dwelling, was viewed as domestic space requiring special attention to its maintenance and cleanliness. The family complex was the scene of activity from dawn to dark. Brothers and sisters performed routine daily tasks. Sisters prepared meals, cleaned the dwelling, washed and mended clothing, and carried out other domestic responsibilities. Brothers cared for livestock, cut and hauled firewood, maintained the buildings, and performed heavier jobs. Children, if part of the family unit, participated in these chores and performed other lesser duties.

In 1768 the Moravians in Salem, North Carolina, broke ground for the new Single Brothers' House. Late the next year, the single men moved into their new home, which included workshops as well as living quarters. By 1786, however, the house was too small, and the Brothers built an addition, doubling the size of the building.

The rooms were extremely simple. This view of the hall shows six of the workshops. The white sack on the floor outside the weaver's shop contains yarn. The barrels are outside the coopers' shop.

Two graceful wrought-iron rat-tail hinges affix the door to this walnut map cupboard, now in Old Salem collections. The rat-tail hinge enables the door to be easily removed when one is moving the piece, and thus has a functional purpose in addition to being a pleasing form.

The rat-tail hinge has its roots in European furniture, and is fairly common on Moravian furniture made in the eighteenth century.

49

The Gentleman Farmers

Shirley Plantation, was built in Charles City County, Virginia, in 1738. John Carter III, the eldest son and principal heir of Robert "King" Carter of Corotoman, one of early Virginia's wealthiest planters, erected an extraordinary and certainly unique group of buildings at Shirley, his wife's estate, which he also inherited. At the center of a strict geometrical layout of house and dependencies is the three-story mansion, forty-eight feet square and nearly a cube, an original design in the Anglo-Dutch style so prominently introduced at the Governor's Palace in Williamsburg. While the original main entrance to the house was originally on the James River side, modern visitors make their entry from the land side. Shirley Plantation demonstrates eighteenth-century Virginians' audacious attempts to simulate the grand lifestyle of the London gentry in order to prove their cultural sophistication. Their efforts reveal the unique position of Virginia's frontier society as allied with England, yet far from identical to it.

In a rare feat of historical survival, Shirley Plantation has remained a working farm owned by the same family since 1660. The current occupants represent the tenth and eleventh generations of Carters on this land. Its double porticoes, added by John Carter III's son after 1771, replaced original stone steps and the gauged brick surrounds of a once flat façade. Flanking the house at distances of thirty-six feet, were equally tall three-story, single-pile long houses, destroyed in the nineteenth century and only recently excavated. Their dimensions of twenty-four by sixty feet are also multiples of the number twelve, the mathematical key to the mansion complex, all of which was probably designed by a creative architect.

The monumental white columns of the Palladian porticoes indicate clearly how the colony's warm climate shaped the development of Georgian architecture in the region. A columned portico was also an architectural proclamation of southern wealth and pride.

Shirley's famed "flying walnut" staircase zigzags three stories overhead in the front hall, supported by a carefully concealed system of cantilevers. For the very wealthy, isolated on their plantations, entertaining had become a significant activity as early as the 1680s, when Virginians were said never to have "anything to do except make visits to their neighbors." In the 1690s some Virginians even dared to criticize Governor Nicholson for serving only one dish of meat at his table. As early as 1705, according to Robert Beverley, they dined "as at the best tables in London" and offered hospitality unmatched in the world. Over the next two decades, as they "improved in . . . polite living," their drinking and dining vessels—of costly silver, ceramic, and glass, as listed in their inventories—multiplied in number, and the ceremony of dining became a formal domestic ritual. Until the last quarter of the eighteenth century, when a separate dining room and a separate parlor came into vogue, a single room, the best in the house—large, well appointed, and prominently positioned—was given to that ritual. It was an outgrowth of the old multipurpose hall.

Over the mantel in the dining room of Shirley is a portrait of Elizabeth Carter, the wife of William Byrd III of Westover, by John Wollaston. In May 1854, Julia Tyler, the wife of the tenth president of the United States (who was himself a Virginia gentleman) visited Shirley and wrote to her mother: "'Shirley' is indeed a fine old place, but if it were mine I should arrange it so differently. I should at least have the parlour in better taste and in conformity with modern fashion. Old and fine portraits all round the rooms for four generations back and coats of arms are over two doors in the hall as in old English style. It seemed like perfect affectation, or dislike to spend money, or bad taste that everything should remain so old fashioned, even to the fixtures of the tea and breakfast tables, and yet there was a crowd of every necessary thing—and yet it cannot be on account of the expense that no change is made where it can be avoided, as we know how liberal are the Carters in other respects." Mrs. Tyler's mid-nineteenth-century letter documents the remarkable fact that many of Shirley's eighteenth-century treasures are still exactly where she saw them. It also confirms the modern visitor's impression that the house is a genuine survival rather than a studied reconstruction. Shirley is located on the James River, twenty miles south of Richmond.

Gunston Hall on Mason's Neck, Virginia, was the home of Revolutionary patriot George Mason, author of the Virginia Declaration of Rights and much of the 1776 constitution of Virginia. Mason's home overlooking the Potomac River is one of the nation's most noted examples of Colonial architecture. The compact plain-brick exterior was constructed around 1755.

William Buckland, a skilled English architect and joiner, designed the extraordinarily rich interiors, including a rare Chinese-style dining room. Research indicates that William Bernard Sears, one of Buckland's artisans, crafted the masterful carving and other detailing. The house and its extensive formal gardens present one of America's most elegant expressions of Colonial taste. Gunston Hall is a one-and-a-half story, gable-roofed brick structure, modest in scale and exterior design, except for the quoins that ornament the corners of the building.

In 1755, Buckland was hired to sail to Virginia and, working as an indentured servant, to design and supervise construction of the interiors of Gunston Hall. The twenty-two-year old flaunted his talent by embellishing the interior with fabulous wooden ornaments carved in the classical and Chinese tastes. In 1759, at the end of Buckland's term of service, George Mason commended him as "a complete master of the Carpenter's and Joiner's Business both in theory and practice." Buckland's career in Virginia ended in 1772 when he moved to Maryland.

The Palladian Parlor of Gunston Hall was probably used almost exclusively to entertain guests. Its elaborate woodwork reflects its important status in the hierarchy of rooms. Buckland's designs reflect many features of the British Palladian style. The young craftsman-designer transformed Mason's provincial with fashionable woodwork of exemplary design and craftsmanship. He gathered local carvers and carpenters to form a team that was active in Virginia's Northern Neck throughout the 1760s. As Gunston Hall aptly illustrates, sophisticated North Americans respected architectural proportion principles as well.

This doctrine of décor or propriety, was rooted in Vitruvius and legislated the issue of correctness: In the most formal places, one must employ an orthodox handling of the orders and their appendages. Following this tenet of propriety, Buckland basically graded the orders at Gunston Hall from the Doric for the most public and formal areas, through the Ionic, and to the Corinthian for the most festive apartment. Washington and Jefferson must have sat here and discussed the important issues of the day with George Mason.

The northeast bedchamber on the first floor of Gunston Hall not only served as the Masons' bedroom, but it was truly the center of operations for the domestic management of the plantation. Ann Eilbeck Mason, mother of nine surviving of twelve children, managed many facets of plantation life from this bedchamber. Here she stored spices, condiments, and foodstuffs, which she gave to the servants as needed. John Mason, a son, records that his mother kept "the smaller or precious stores for the Table" in the closet to the left of the fireplace. Here she also kept the "green doctor," a green leather riding crop with a silver handle, which she used to discipline her nine children.

Mason's land holdings totaled more than 5,000 acres and were divided into four quarters, with Gunston Hall serving as the center of operations. A portion of the land was leased to tenants who mainly raised tobacco. On the acreage that Mason farmed, he cultivated corn and wheat in addition to tobacco. Where the tester bed is now placed in this bedchamber, there was once a servants' staircase occupying the corner of the room. The stairs originated in the basement, opened into the side hall passage on the first floor, and into the hall on the second floor. Thus, the servants could access the second floor of the mansion without disturbing the Mason family in the hall, parlor, and dining room.

55

Wilton, in Richmond, Virginia, was built between 1750 and 1753 for William Randolph III on a high bluff overlooking the James River, some fifteen miles from its present site. The original plantation had two offices, a storehouse, and a dairy and kitchen as outbuildings. Always a well-known house but frequently neglected, it was described by one visitor in 1833 as being in "such ruin; Broken down fences, a falling piazza, defaced paint, banisters tied up with ropes, etc." In 1933, the Colonial Dames took title to Wilton, moved it to its new site, and restored and furnished it. Its exterior has some of the finest brickwork in the state, while its interior is paneled from floor to ceiling in every room.

With its regular five-bay façades and geometric proportions, Wilton is a superb essay in Colonial design. This example of the symmetrical Georgian style reflects the dignified conservatism of the Colonial aristocracy. The house is capped by a low-pitched, hipped roof, and its brick façade is enlivened by edgings of vermilion-rubbed brick at the corners and around the windows and doorway. George Washington stayed as a guest at Wilton in 1775 after attending the Richmond Convention, where Patrick Henry delivered his fiery challenge "Give me liberty, or give me death!"

The parlor of Wilton features arches, molded keystones, a pulvinated frieze, and twelve fluted pilasters. The construction of Wilton may have been undertaken by Richard Taliaferro, a planter-builder of Powhatan plantation near Williamsburg, who was lauded by Thomas Lee, president of the Governor's Council, as "our most skillful architect." Taliaferro repaired and enlarged the Governor's Palace from 1752 to 1754 and built a handsome, two-story, hip-roofed house on the Green at Williamsburg for his daughter and her husband, the lawyer George Wythe, in about 1755. The parlor paneling recalls the late baroque style of the British architect Sir Christopher Wren and his master carver, Grinling Gibbons. Such architectural details as fluted pilasters, arched alcoves, and a finely carved cornice combine to create a sense of movement.

When Wilton was moved and reassembled in 1933, a penciled graffito was discovered left by one of the original carpenters: "Samson Daril put up this cornish in the year of our Lord 1753."

For the interior of Wilton, the builder William Randolph III commissioned superb floor-to-ceiling paneling for every room of the house, including the closets, which were themselves something of an extravagance at the time. Lavish in its extent, but subtle in its design, Wilton's paneling hints at wealth without proclaiming it too loudly. "Methodical nicety . . . is the essence of true elegance," wrote a Randolph woman in *The Virginia Housewife*, a book about household management. That sentiment describes Wilton exactly.

A bedroom at Wilton.

A Gatefold of Eighteenth Century Windows, Stairways and Doors

Opposite, right

A view from the window above the main entrance of Poplar Hall, near Dover, Delaware, the home of John Dickinson. The house was begun in 1740 by Dickinson's father. It was rebuilt in 1804 after a fire. Dickinson was one of America's leading lawyers and articulated the colonists' sentiments about taxation without representation.

LETTERS
FROM A
FARMER in PENSILVANIA,
TO THE
INHABITANTS
OF THE
BRITISH COLONIES.

[Price Two Shillings.]

Above
The front doorway of the Sheldon-Hawks House in Deerfield, Massachusetts, built about 1743. The triangular pedimented Connecticut River Valley doorway was probably added to the house about 1760. These architectural embellishments were produced by a handful of house joiners who plied their trade up and down the valley between about 1750 and 1790.

Opposite, left
In eighteenth-century New England, houses typically had staircases that looked like the above, rather than the one in the Silas Dean house on the far right. This simpler version at Strawberry Banke in New Hampshire would have been the work of an artisan called a "joiner," one who joined boards, panels, and frames to create simple interior architecture.

Three Newburyport, Massachusetts doorways:
Above are the double doors of the Knight-Short House.

The entrance hall of Wright's Ferry Mansion evokes seventeenth-century design with its brick floor, massive Dutch doors at each end, and magnificent staircase with turned balusters.

One of the windows on the east side of the house of Quaker botanist John Bartram. Located on the west bank of the Schuylkill River, the house is built of local stone (Wissahickon schist), which he quarried himself and carved with rough simulations or Georgian console brackets and Ionic columns—showing that Bartram was familiar with eighteenth-century English design books. He would later recount that he had "split rocks, seventeen feet long, and built four houses of hewn stone split out of the rock with my own hands."

A protuding brick-colored keystone above the open doorway of the Spencer-Pierce-Little farmhouse.

The simple transomed later doorway of the 1636 Atkinson House.

Opposite, right
The elegant staircase that Silas Deane ordered in 1766 for his new house in Wethersfield, Connecticut, is a marvel of the woodturner's art. Each tread has three different baluster patterns. The most striking is the corkscrewlike "twisted" turning, characteristic of the English Cromwellian period but rare in America. This illustrates the lag of fashion between England and New England—the height of the Cromwellian period had been a hundred years earlier.

Opposite, left

The mahogany double stairway in Drayton Hall. The plan of Drayton Hall is similar to that of Chester Lee-Street, a house designed by Colen Campbell and published by him in *Vitruvius Britannicus* (1717). The fully paneled stair hall, which rises a magnificent twenty-seven feet, is the finest in America. The balusters on the double staircase, with bulbous rather than straight Doric columns, are most unusual. Remarkably, the family never added plumbing, electric lighting, or central heating, and the house remains much as it was in the eighteenth century.

Opposite, right
A detail of the stairway
at Wilton, Virginia.

Kenmore, Fredericksburg, Virginia, 1775–1776. Kenmore is one of America's most noted works of Georgian architecture, and has gained renown for the lavishness of its plasterwork. The house was completed by 1776 for Fielding Lewis and his wife, Betty Washington Lewis, the only sister of George Washington. The Lewises built Kenmore on land surveyed for them twenty-five years earlier by Washington. Lewis was a merchant and planter as well as a Revolutionary patriot. He served in the Virginia House of Burgesses, financed the Fredericksburg Gun Manufactory, and helped organize local resistance against the British by merchants and militia. The Lewises' brick mansion, with its plain but formal exterior, boasts an exceptionally elaborate interior with the finest eighteenth-century plasterwork ceilings and chimneypieces in the country. Fielding Lewis built his house on a hill overlooking his wharves and ships in the port of Fredericksburg. Taking on a role that was high unusual for the era, Betty Lewis participated as a partner with her husband in their business ventures. In addition to financing and managing the gun factory, the Lewises built and provisioned ships, and provided gunpowder, clothing, food, and other supplies to Washington's army. Exhausted by constant work, Fielding Lewis died impoverished after Washington's victory at Yorktown in 1781.

preceding page

The craftsman who executed this elaborate plasterwork in the drawing room remains anonymous, but Fielding Lewis referred to him as a "Frenchman" when writing in 1775, annoyed with his brother-in-law George Washington, about the length of time the work was taking. According to correspondence at Mount Vernon, the same Frenchman also worked on the interior there.

At Kenmore, the drawing room, dining room, and master bedroom are covered with the elaborate plasterwork of the itinerant Frenchman, a "stucco man" who favored floral motifs. The plasterwork overmantel for this room depicts a scene from Aesop's fable of the fox and the crow, which dramatizes the moral "beware of flattery."

A door handle at Kenmore. Designs like these were often used for knockers.

The intricately carved wooden mantel of the dining room bears the Washington crest, a swan and a crown, among leafy scrolls. This carving is associated with the work attributed to George Hamilton, a carver and gilder who left London in April 1774, listed on customs records as a twenty-five-year-old native of Scotland. In July of that year he was in Williamsburg, advertising from the cabinetmaking shop established by Anthony Hay: "George Hamilton, Carver and Gilder, just from Britain, and now in this City." He claimed to be working in the latest "Palmyrian taste" in his architectural work. Pendant husks and anthemions used in the Kenmore carving illustrate the Palmyrian, or neoclassical, style, a lighter, more domestic version of classical design influenced by the excavations of Pompeii and Herculaneum, and popularized in England in the 1760s by architect Robert Adam.

The walls of this bedchamber at Kenmore have been repainted the original Pompeian red. The corner sections of the plasterwork ceiling are ornamented with plants that symbolize each of the four seasons—palms for spring, grapes for summer, acorns for autumn, and mistletoe for winter. The side chairs are from Philadelphia, made about 1775. Fielding and Betty Lewis engaged in a variety of economic enterprises, giving them some protection against the vagaries of the tobacco trade, and it appeared that they would lead a quiet and prosperous life at Kenmore. During the 1760s, however, drastic declines in the prices received for tobacco, coupled with import duties imposed by the Townshend Acts, began to create financial problems for Virginians. Pressed by what they saw as unfair and punitive policies, Fielding Lewis and his brother-in-law George Washington gradually turned against the British crown. During the Revolution, Fielding Lewis oversaw Washington's estates as well as his own, and between 1775 and his death in 1781, Lewis financed and helped operate a gun manufactory in Fredericksburg. The war destroyed the economy and currency of Virginia, and Fielding Lewis died embittered and impoverished.

Republican and Palladian

As can be seen with his home Mount Vernon, in Alexandria, Virginia, George Washington's enduring fame as a general and statesman has overshadowed his achievement as an amateur architect. In 1761 he inherited the modest farmhouse built by his father on the family's Mount Vernon plantation, located on a bluff over the Potomac River. In stages, Washington transformed the plain structure into a grand manor, imposing on the outside and boasting one of the most elegant interiors in Virginia. Self-sufficiency, agrarianism, and republicanism were fundamental beliefs of Washington and his contemporaries, so it was to the classical design theories of Andrea Palladio that he turned when he began to enlarge Mount Vernon. Then, in the 1780s, Washington adopted the new decorative style of Robert Adam, which provided a classical framework for the symbolism of the new republic. For Washington and his generation, ideas about farming, architecture, decoration, and political ideology were interrelated to a degree that is difficult for the twenty-first-century mind to comprehend. In his first rebuilding of 1758 to 1763, Washington raised the dwelling to two stories and an attic, and he developed the geometric layout adjacent to the house. The sweeping second rebuilding of 1774 to 1787 roughly doubled the length of the house while increasing the height to three stories. It added the celebrated east "piazza," the cupola, the west pediment, and the arcaded quadrants leading to two new western outbuildings.

Though Washington himself referred to his plain "republican style of living," he had a taste for grandeur and large-scale architectural statements. The major architectural problem he faced in Mount Vernon was the asymmetry of the doors and windows on both the west and the east, or river, façades. While this problem was never completely solved, it prompted a number of ingenious changes. The entire house was sheathed with pine boards deeply scored to look like blocks of stone. White lead paint was then applied and, while still wet, sand was thrown against it to simulate the texture of stone. The rustication created a pattern that quite effectively obscures the asymmetry of the fenestration. Washington flanked the house with irregular groves overlooking the Potomac, and he replaced the geometric western approach with an "English garden": a bowling green set within a serpentine walk, "shrubberies," and "wildernesses" which screened out utilitarian structures and areas laid out formally behind them. He also replaced most of the outbuildings, an enterprise that continued into the 1790s. Arriving at Mount Vernon's gate, visitors gaze across an expansive lawn toward the broad white mansion that evokes, as the architect Benjamin Henry Latrobe put it, "a plain English country gentleman's house . . . of the old school."

Acquired over a period of forty years from a variety of sources, new and used, foreign and domestic, his household possessions came together harmoniously at the end of his life as the culmination of his sense of beauty, order, and dignity and as a reflection of taste and American craftsmanship in the early years of the republic. The large, elegant, neoclassical dining room was furnished in 1797 with twenty-four mahogany side chairs made by the cabinetmaker John Aitken of Philadelphia.

From its raising in 1776, the two-story dining room (or "New Room") that occupies the entire north addition was conceived by Washington as the grandest public room at Mount Vernon. Although it was not completed until 1788, Washington and the French generals planned the Battle of Yorktown in this room in 1781. It was here too that Washington received word that he had been elected the first president of the United States, and it was here in 1799 that his body lay in state for three days before burial. The form of this room belongs to the same British Palladian genre as the cove-ceilinged Double-Cube Room at Wilton House (1648–1650) in Wiltshire, England, which had become a dining room by the early eighteenth century. Inigo Jones had introduced the "cubic" proportional system in the Vitruvian tradition to the English-speaking world in the seventeenth century, but such proportions became popular only later, in the eighteenth century. George Washington, the statesman and gentleman-architect who gave shape to Mount Vernon, very likely meant his room to follow the arithmetic progression of 2, 3, and 4.

This is the most Adamesque of all the rooms at Mount Vernon, incorporating the expanded repertory of classical forms and the use of many colors that Robert Adam created after the influential discovery of the ruins of Pompeii and Herculaneum. The new low-relief ornaments could almost all be executed in plaster or composition, making them considerably less expensive than early Palladian and rococo ornaments, which required skilled wood carvers and plasterworkers. The decorative techniques represented in the room include cast and plasterwork, composition ornament, wood fretwork and moldings, paint, wallpaper, and printed-paper borders. Washington's English admirer, Samuel Vaughn, sent him a marble mantel for the room, which is now the centerpiece of the south wall. Vaughn had the mantel removed from his own house in England and shipped to Mount Vernon. Fashioned of marble with fluted columns of brown jasper, the mantel features three panels carved with farming scenes. The room is hung with landscape views of the Hudson and Potomac rivers. They are related to the paintings of Claude Lorraine, which would have decorated a comparable English interior. Mount Vernon was described by one eighteenth-century traveler as "a country house of an elegant and majestic simplicity."

Doorway in the large dining room at Mount Vernon. Washington himself planned some of the decoration in the large dining room. He wrote to Clement Biddle in 1784: "I have seen rooms with gilded borders; made of I believe papier mache fastened on which Brads or Cement round the Doors and window casings, surbase, &c.; and which gives a plain blew or green paper a rich and handsome look." The printed architectural border may be among the first to have been used in the United States, since such borders were relatively new in Europe in the 1780s.

George Washington's Study. On a visit in 1782 Baron Ludwig von Closen found the "manor-house at Mount Vernon is very spacious, well planned, attractively furnished, and wonderfully well maintained, without ostentation." In his selection of furniture, as in the design of his house, Washington preferred stylish simplicity to ostentatious display.

The small dining room underwent great changes during Washington's own lifetime. They were probably initiated by a change in the configuration of the room when the adjacent study was built in 1775. Choosing a design for the chimneypiece, Washington returned to a plate in Abraham Swan's *British Architect* and employed two extraordinary craftsmen to ensure the faithful replication of the splendid rococo ornament. Bernard Sears was the wood carver and an unnamed Frenchman did the plasterwork.

The anonymous French "stucco man" was also working at the time for Washington's brother-in-law Fielding Lewis at Kenmore in Fredericksburg. The plaster decoration of the chimney piece, cornice, and ceiling is remarkable for its execution and state of preservation. Many of the decorative elements in the ceiling of the small dining room are also found in the more elaborate ceilings at Kenmore. Because the fireplace smoked, the whitewashed walls of the room were painted this brilliant verdigris green in 1785.

73

Thomas Jefferson spent forty years constructing, tearing down, and reconstructing his revolutionary vision of a house, Monticello, in Charlottesville, Virginia. The Duc de La Rochefoucauld-Liancourt, visiting Jefferson in June 1796, found him in the midst of remodeling and enlarging Monticello. There was to be a dome—the first on a house in America—and the apartments, according to the duke, were to be "large and convenient; the decoration, both outside and inside, simple, yet regular and elegant." Jefferson began building Monticello in 1769 when he was twenty-six years old, partly completing a two-story house derived from designs in Andrea Palladio's *Four Books of Architecture*. But when the new U.S. government sent him to France for five years (1784–1789), he had received his first chance to see ancient Roman architecture with his own eyes. He also, in his words, became "violently smitten" by a newly built residence in Paris, the Hôtel de Salm. "All the new and good houses," he wrote of the places he had seen in France, "are of a single story." After his return to Virginia, he tore apart much of what he ad built and undertook the creation of a new Monticello, situated on a mountaintop with sweeping views of the central Virginia countryside.

Monticello is more than just a house and home. In Jefferson's lifetime it was a plantation, or more accurately the head farm of a group of five, comprising 5,000 forested acres in Virginia's Southwest Mountains. Jefferson had, for a time, a mill on the Rivanna River that flowed in the valley below, as well as simple household manufactories in small shops along Mulberry Row, east of the mansion. Of these, the joinery was particularly distinguished. Some of Jefferson's guests found the house too idiosyncratic for their tastes. All agreed, however, on the magnificence of the panoramic spectacle seen from the mountaintop. Here, too, Monticello expressed the mind and temperament of the builder. In William Wirt's classic description: "It stands upon an elliptic plain, formed by cutting down the apex of the mountain, and to the west, stretching away to the north and the south, it commands a view of the Blue Ridge for 150 miles, and brings under the eye one of the boldest and most beautiful horizons in the world; while on the east it presents an extent of prospect bounded only by the spherical form of the earth, in which Nature seems to sleep in eternal repose, as if to form one of the finest contrasts with the rude and rolling grandeur of the west."

For Jefferson, the "first principles" of architecture were founded on the ancient Roman orders. From the beginning of his architectural activity to the culmination of that activity at the end of his life, he treated buildings as opportunities to display examples of the best orders. Jefferson disdained what he regarded as the crude simplicity of Colonial Virginia's brick buildings, which reminded him of British rule. For Monticello, he devised a complex but harmonious geometry of circles, triangles, and octagons. On April 13, 1782, Jefferson, then governor of Virginia, welcomed to Monticello a distinguished guest, the Chevalier de Chastellux. It happened to be Jefferson's thirty-ninth birthday. Chastellux, a member of the French Academy, had traveled westward from Williamsburg, where he was stationed with General Rochambeau's victorious army. His literary portrait of Jefferson presented him to the world in philosophical colors. It was enhanced by placing him in the context of the remarkable house this Virginian had raised on the mountaintop in Albemarle County: "Mr. Jefferson is the first American who has consulted the Fine Arts to know how he should shelter himself from the weather."

Poplar Forest, Bedford County, Virginia, 1806–1825.
Jefferson never ceased to be an active architect. No sooner was Monticello finished than he began to build an amazing single-story octagonal house at his Bedford County retreat or "heritage," Poplar Forest, eighty miles south. He demonstrated an almost inordinate fondness for polygonal and octagonal rooms throughout his architectural career. At Poplar Forest he went a step further by designing a completely octagonal house. Around a central cubical dining room lit only by a skylight are a series of small rooms—some octagonal, some polygonal. The two main bedrooms, east and west of the dining room, originally contained central-alcove beds, another favorite of Jefferson's. To the south is an elongated octagonal parlor flooded with sunlight from windows facing southeast and southwest as well as south.

To mitigate the heat and intense glare of summer, the windows facing directly south are shaded by a porch. At sixty-eight years old and retired from the presidency for two years, Jefferson wrote to his friend Dr. Benjamin Rush in the summer of 1811: "I write to you from a place, 90 miles from Monticello . . . which I visit three or four times a year. I stay from a fortnight to a month at a time. I have fixed myself comfortably, keep some books here, bring others occasionally, am in the solitude of a hermit, and quite at leisure to attend to my absent friends."

On the issue of architectural authority, which means the claims of the "ancients" versus the "moderns," Jefferson preferred the ancients and modeled his buildings on great ancient edifices. Among the "modern" interpreters of antiquity, Palladio was held first in Jefferson's esteem. In 1816, Colonel Isaac A. Coles reported to General John Hartwell Cocke in a letter about a consultation he had with Jefferson: "Palladio he was 'was the Bible.'" Jefferson's architecture grew out of the pattern books of a bookish movement. Benjamin Henry Latrobe, the professional who emphatically did not depend on a library when he designed, paid him a telling, qualified compliment in calling Jefferson an "excellent architect out of books." Jefferson embraced the important ideas on materials and planning offered in Giacomo Leoni's edition of Palladio's *Quattro Libri*. He inveighed against wooden buildings in his *Notes on the State of Virginia* and promoted the masonry wall. Apparently taking the Villa Rotonda as the ideal model for a civil official's house, he became a devotee of the bow window ("They were charming—they gave you a semicircle of air & light") and arrived at—or perhaps invented—a distinctive form, the bow window "caged" inside a temple portico.

The southern breadth of the house was Jefferson's private domain, his "sanctum sanctorum," as an early guest called it. The house held more than 6,000 books, which in 1815 became the nucleus of the Library of Congress. One of Jefferson's granddaughters wrote that "books were at all times his chosen companions . . . I saw him more frequently with a volume of the classics in his hand than with any other book." The books were stored in five different sizes of open wooden boxes with a shelf in the middle. They were stacked by size, with folios on the bottom, followed by quartos, octavos, duodecimos, and petit-format books at the top.

One of the things that attracted Jefferson to Philadelphia and Paris was, undoubtedly, the access that he would have to more cosmopolitan bookstores: "While reading in Paris, I devoted every afternoon I was disengaged, for a summer or two, in examining all the principal bookstores, turning over every book with my own hand, and putting by everything which related to America, and indeed whatever was rare and valuable in every science." He once told John Adams, "I cannot live without books."

Separated from the dining room by double sets of pocket doors is the room Jefferson called his "most honorable suite," the tea room. It contained an outstanding collection of portraits and provided another place where he could read and write. Thirty-four engravings, miniatures, and medals, mainly of Revolutionary War figures, ornamented the polygonal room. Jefferson considered Houdon "without rivalship the first statuary of this age," and assembled eight works by him at Monticello. The tea room was encircled by some of the terra-cotta patinated busts on console brackets. In addition to those of Turgot and Voltaire, there were plaster busts of Jefferson himself, George Washington, Benjamin Franklin, John Paul Jones, the Marquise de Lafayette, and a now lost Diana. Also in the tea room was a bust of General Andrew Jackson by William Rush, which was given to Jefferson in February 1820 by his friend James Ronaldson of Philadelphia. The walls were crowded with reminders of historical events and absent friends.

The dining room received family members and guests for two meals each day, breakfast and dinner. While waiting for his family to gather, Jefferson often sat reading; a visitor noted that "on the mantel-piece . . . were many books of all kinds." Another praised the behavior of Jefferson's grandchildren, who "are in such excellent order, that you would not know, if you did not see them, that a child was present." Because the dining room was located on the cold north side of the house, a window with triple-hung sash was double-glazed to conserve heat. Rather than use a single dining table, Jefferson owned several that could be put together; when not in use, the tables were placed against the walls. Two dumbwaiters, installed on either side of the fireplace, carried bottles of wine from the wine cellar below. In 1819, at the age of seventy-six, he wrote in response to a physician's inquiry about his daily routine: "Like my friend [Dr. Benjamin Rush], I have lived temperately, eating little animal food. . . . I double, however, the Doctor's glass and a half of wine, and even treble it with a friend . . . but halve its effects by drinking the weak wines only."

In his lifetime, Jefferson's art collection ranked among the largest in the United States, although he had little firsthand knowledge of art until he went to Paris in the 1780s. He relished the salon of 1787, with paintings hung in tiers in the Salon Carré of the Musée du Louvre, and he wrote to the U.S. painter John Trumbull that he should not miss it. Monticello was filled with the furnishings, the pictures and sculptures, and the household goods Jefferson had acquired during his five years in Paris. Packed in eighty-six crates, the shipment of goods followed him home. Some of the pieces, considered too formal for a country house, were left behind in Philadelphia when he retired as secretary of state in the new government, but mostly they furnished Monticello. Jefferson's taste in painting approximated the cultivated taste of the time. The subject matter ran to the biblical, the classical, and the biographical. Here, too, his taste was refined in Paris. David was the greatest living painter, he thought, as Houdon was the premier sculptor of the age. Some of the fifty-seven works of art, of which thirty-five were portraits hung in three tiers, can be seen reflected in the parlor mirrors. The likenesses included Jefferson's trinity of the greatest men who ever lived—John Locke, Francis Bacon, and Sir Isaac Newton.

Jefferson's comfortable private quarters consisted of four connected rooms: his bedchamber, cabinet, greenhouse, and book room. Others rarely entered these rooms. His habit was to arise at dawn, "as soon as he can see the hands of his clock, which is directly opposite his bed," Daniel Webster reported in 1824, and examine "the thermometer immediately, as he keeps a regular meteorological diary." Jefferson spent much of the morning and late afternoon reading and answering correspondence in his cabinet, or study. For convenience and comfort, he assembled a reading and writing arrangement in the center of the room that included a revolving chair, a writing table with a rotating top, a Windsor couch for resting his legs, and a revolving bookstand that could hold five open volumes at a time. On top of the writing table was a copying machine called a "polygraph," which duplicated Jefferson's letters as he wrote. Scientific instruments in profusion—telescopes, microscopes, compasses, thermometers, an orrery, theodolite, circumferenter, and micrometer—indicated his "ardent desire to see knowledge disseminated through the mass of mankind."

The double-height bedchamber features an unusual double-sided bed alcove that connects with the cabinet. A crimson silk counterpane, sewn to Jefferson's specifications in 1808, covered his bed. His out-of-season clothing and extra bedcovers were stored in a closet over the bed alcove that could be reached by a ladder. Garments for everyday wear hung on a "turning machine" with forty-eight arms placed at the foot of his bed. Visiting the mountaintop in 1809, Margaret Bayard Smith reported that Jefferson "asked us into what I had called his sanctum sanctorum, into which it is very seldom anyone is admitted." On July 4, 1826, the fiftieth anniversary of the day that Congress approved the Declaration of Independence, Jefferson died in his bed at almost one o'clock in the afternoon. John Adams died later that same day, believing that Jefferson still survived.

A Gatefold of Doorways and Windows

Opposite, right
A Palladian window on the north side of Mount Vernon. Of the several dozen English architectural pattern books that were the product of that nation's Palladian Revival of the early eighteenth century, many made their way by midcentury to the American colonies. These gave professionals and amateurs much easier access than before to countless façade designs, plans, and examples of classical detailing creatively adapted to uses in contemporary interiors and exteriors. So lucid and handsomely engraved are the plates that their designs were implemented in the colonies with enough frequency and skill to instill in the more costly American buildings a new aura of sophisticated—though still provincial—formality. Instances in Virginia of direct reference to plates in pattern books are well known. Mount Vernon, whose owner, George Washington, is known to have been personally involved in designing the intricacies of the building, is a repository of examples of sourcebook adaptations. The Palladian window shown follows a design in Batty Langley's *Treasury of Designs* (London, 1740, plate 51), probably the same source as for the Tuscan piers of Mount Vernon's two-story piazza.

The parlor at sunset. Rarely in history has a great man encompassed himself so completely in his domicile as Jefferson at Monticello. President Franklin D. Roosevelt, a frequent visitor, once wrote admiringly: "More than any historic home in America, Monticello appeals to me as an expression of the personality of its builder. In the design, not of the whole alone, but of every room, of every part of every room, in the very furnishings which Jefferson devised on his own drawing board and made in his own workshop, there speaks ready capacity for detail and, above all, creative genius." Reading Jefferson through his house, the writer John Dos Passos thought that Monticello was a corollary of the Declaration of Independence: "A house where a free man could live in a society of equals."

The open doorway of Rosedown, in Louisiana, looks out to the extensive gardens described on page 160.

Right
The light-filled entrance hall at Monticello was used by Jefferson as the reception area and also as a "cabinet" to impress visitors with his collection of North American natural history specimens.

The hall of Hope Plantation, in North Carolina, was used as a living room in the summer. The home was built in the early 1800s by its owner, David Stone, using cypress and pine from his surrounding land, cut at his own sawmill.

The four panes in the transom above the front door of the Old Manse in
Concord, Massachusetts, are made of bulls-eye glass. This attractive effect was
the result of early glass-making techniques. Molten glass was spun out as a
large flat lollipop and the thick distorted center was used by the less well-off
for their windows, or for transoms and side lights.

A kitchen of the 1840s is seen from a doorway at the historic Tullie-Smith farm in Georgia. Because of heat from the open hearth and the danger of fire, many kitchens in the South were detached from the main house.

This view of a double-crib 1845 Tennessee farmhouse at the Homeplace looks into the main living area, through the open hall, and beyond into the kitchen. The open hall was known as a "dog trot" and joined the two cribs or "pens" on either side. The dog trot was favored in the South because it made an airy, cooler place for the family to eat or do chores in warm weather.

Opposite, left

The splendid entrance to the Hammond-Harwood House in Annapolis, Maryland, testifies to the skill and vision of William Buckland, an English architect who received his training in London and then came to the colonies in 1755 as an indentured servant. This house is the last of his architectural commissions. The house was built in 1774 and 1775 by Mathias Hammond, a young lawyer and patriot. He intended this "elegant and commodious" residence to be his town house, in which he could further his political career and enjoy the winter social and legislative session, which lasted from November through January or February. Hammond spent most of the year at his house in the country, as did most other people of means in Annapolis.

The house's overall proportions so pleased Thomas Jefferson when he visited the town that he sketched the facade for his future reference. The house remains one of the most accomplished—and most English—of America's Colonial houses.

Stratford Hall, overlooking the Potomac River in Westmoreland County, Virginia, was built by Thomas Lee about 1738. Lee's massive mansion adapts the baroque monumentality of the English school of Sir John Vanburgh and Nicholas Hawksmoor to the region's climate, building materials, and social needs. It uses an *H*-plan, a Jacobean type that had been recently revived in English Georgian houses, but local Colonial architecture was just as likely an influence—at the first Virginia capitol, Lee had experienced the generous lighting and ventilation of a large *H*-plan building. In its two wings, Lee's *H*-plan provided abundant space for the activities important to his generation of Virginians. The two largest rooms on the upper floor of the garden wing were given to dining and sitting. Four cool bedchambers were located on the ground floor of the more private back wing. Stratford, an original creation, clearly speaks of the high status of its owner, the extent of his hospitality, and to our modern eyes, his vigorous, provincial spirit.

Few places in America equal Stratford in architectural interest or historical association. The builder, Thomas Lee, served in Virginia's House of Burgesses and as the colony's acting governor. In 1744 he was one of Britain's chief negotiators in talks with the Six Nations of the Iroquois that resulted in the acquisition of enormous territories in the West—lands that later formed six states and part of a seventh. His sons stood in the forefront of the patriots' cause in the era of the Revolution. John Adams called the Lees "this band of brothers, intrepid and unchangeable." Richard Henry Lee and Francis Lightfoot Lee signed the Declaration of Independence—the only brothers among the signers. William Lee and Arthur Lee served as diplomats in Europe, and Thomas Lee held a post in Virginia's Revolutionary government. Through marriage, Stratford Hall came into the possession of a cousin, Henry "Light Horse Harry" Lee, one of the great cavalry heroes of the Revolution. His second wife, Ann Carter of Shirley Plantation, gave birth to five children, including Robert Edward Lee in 1807.

At the center of the house and on the piano nobile is the great hall of Stratford. The hall, 29 1/2 feet square, with a 16 1/2-foot coved ceiling and ornately decorated with Corinthian pilasters, is one of the most handsome rooms created in Colonial America.

Each of the four large windows has a window seat and folding shutters. Double doors at the north and south open to the outside; those on the east and west lead to wide passages floored with pine boards some thirty feet long.

Used only in the summer, the hall has no fireplaces. Beginning about 1720, a thriving market in English architectural handbooks offered a potpourri of classical elements from which a house builder could assemble a unique expression of his individual taste and personality. The opulence and grandeur that often resulted not only announced one's enormous economic success but also expressed a desire to bring Virginia, seen as a cultural backwater, into the intellectual mainstream.

The Federal mahogany desk-and-bookcase in the parlor at Stratford was made in Salem, Massachusetts, and once belonged to General Robert E. Lee, a descendant of Thomas Lee. It is one of the few Lee family pieces now in the house. In 1829 Lee graduated from the U.S. Military Academy second in his class and received a commission in the Engineer Corps. Two years later he married Mary Custis, heir to Arlington Plantation. His skill and daring in the Mexican War won him the admiration of Winfield Scott and a promotion to brevet colonel. From 1852 to 1855 Lee was superintendent of West Point. During the secession crisis in 1861, he declined an offer of principal field command from Scott and followed Virginia into the Confederacy.

Called the "American Napoleon," Lee displayed audacity and initiative in his zeal to "strike a blow" as an offensive commander. His use of trenches to offset his inferior numbers proved his genius on the defense. He has remained an American hero—revered for his strength of character and the brilliance of his battles.

The bedchamber at Stratford Hall is known as "Mother's Room." The mistress of the house occupied this large bedroom, which was the hub of the plantation; here she gave orders to the servants and bore her children. The late-eighteenth-century mahogany bed may have been made in Charleston, South Carolina. The fabric used throughout the room is a reproduction of a toile de Jouy from about 1750, an American homage to France. Robert E. Lee slept in the crib in front of the window after his birth on January 19, 1807. The future general spent his early childhood here, but the family departed in 1822 when failed land speculations ruined Henry Lee financially, compelling him to chain the doors of the house to keep out the collectors. He was eventually imprisoned for his debts. After passing through several owners in the nineteenth century, the property was acquired in 1929 by the Robert E. Lee Memorial Association. The restored plantation is now an historic site interpreting Colonial plantation life and the Lee family.

Drayton Hall on the Ashley River in the Carolina Low Country. The construction of this Georgian-Palladian plantation house was begun in 1738 by the Honorable John Drayton, a member of His Majesty's Council, and completed in 1742. Drayton Hall, said to have cost $90,000, is built of brick in Flemish bond. The double portico of Doric and Ionic columns on the west façade was inspired by Andrea Palladio's *I quattro libri dell' architettura*, published in Venice in 1570, in which numerous examples of such porticoes are illustrated. Because this type of portico is airy and open, it became a favorite in the Low Country and in Charleston as well. The builder's son, William Henry Drayton, became the Revolutionary Chief Justice of South Carolina. This is the only plantation house along the Ashley River to survive the Civil War. It is said that its owner, Dr. Charles Drayton, had his slaves tell Union soldiers that the house was being used as a smallpox hospital, and no soldier dared come near it. The garden at Drayton Hall has disappeared, but the Duc de la Rochefoucauld-Liancourt, who visited the plantation in the spring of 1796, found it handsome: "The house is an ancient building, but convenient and good; and the garden is better laid out, better cultivated and stocked with good trees, than any I have hitherto seen. In order to have a fine garden you have nothing to do but to let the trees remain standing here and there, or in clumps, to plant bushes in front of them, and arrange the trees according to their height." The house remained in the Drayton family for seven generations until purchased by the National Trust for Historic Preservation in 1974.

The progression of classical orders in the three main rooms in the house is adopted from Greek architecture. In the great hall, or reception room, on the first floor are Doric pilasters; in the Ionic room, the small south parlor overlooking the river, are Ionic pilasters; and in the drawing room on the second floor are Corinthian pilasters. Tongue-and-groove wooden ceilings replaced the original plaster ones through the second floor when the house was reconditioned after the Civil War. The ceiling in this room is fourteen feet high. A member of the Drayton family painted the coat of arms in the overmantel in the 1930s. The interiors survive architecturally in almost their original condition, and this fact, plus their superb quality, makes them one of the great treasures of eighteenth-century American art.

The Nineteenth- and Early-Twentieth-Century American House

James Howard Kunstler

In 1804, Charles Culver had a long wooden ropewalk in which he successfully produced rigging for local sailing vessels, located in New London, Connecticut. His business was destroyed by fire and he sold the narrow piece of land as real estate development.

A narrow street was created, named after the C. Starr and Company Soap and Candle Factory. The factory was at one end and narrow building lots were sold. The houses were erected right on the street line with little space between them.

In the early 1800s, architects were rare in America but a good carpenter could copy or adapt a plan from the available French or English architectural books. In 1839, a John Bishop built five of the houses on Starr Street.

Now known as "Bishop's row," the five identical houses all have a simple entablature beneath the pediment which faces the street, fan windows in the pediment, and a front doorway on the right-hand side with lights above. As in most inner cities, time brought deterioration. In the 1970s, Starr Street's homes were scheduled for demolition under the Federal Redevelopment Program.

The Savings Bank of New London took the controversial step of buying most of the houses, and began a program of accurately restoring the exteriors, while bringing the buildings up to code and adapting the interiors for modern use.

The city of New London contributed to the project by placing utilities underground and installing dry wells, brick sidewalks, and period street lights.

THE FREESTANDING SINGLE-FAMILY HOUSE on a large lot so firmly embedded in our national mythology is a peculiar product of history. At its finest, which was frequently, the American house of a century-and-then-some ago was a fabulous dwelling place for the imagination. In these days of relentlessly sub-mediocre architecture, set within the greater ghastly context of our national automobile slum, it is almost impossible to reflect on the historic American house without a painful sense of longing and regret.

In Europe generally before 1800 and in England in particular, freestanding houses were occupied either by the rich (palaces and country villas) or by rural peasants (cottages and hovels), while the middle class, which had been expanding steadily for centuries, crowded into cities and town centers. Industrialism altered these long-established patterns, and the rise of the American nation coincided with industrialism. Two other elements also converged to produce the American house: cheap land on an expanding frontier, and a seemingly inexhaustible supply of wood for building.

In New England, with its growing merchant class, a vernacular building culture rapidly arose that took neoclassical decorative conventions from masonry architecture—pilasters, corbels, moldings, arched windows—and applied them with great skill using carpentry. Manuals such as Asher Benjamin's *American Builder's Companion* systematized these procedures and made them available to any housewright with a head for figures. Plentiful rural land, meanwhile, promoted a development pattern that favored isolated homesteads, or at least large lots beyond the center of town. The plantation house of the South, the Hudson Valley farmhouse pictured in paintings by Thomas Cole and Jasper Cropsey, the little house on the prairie, the cabin in the woods, all are prototypes within this pattern. Jefferson's Monticello is the archetype, with an overlay of democratic monumentalism that gives the "American Dream" such potency as a cultural icon.

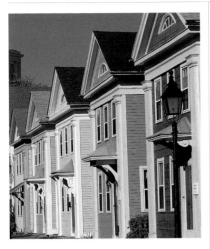

"Bishop's row" in New London

In 1828, a Connecticut architect named Ithiel Town started the fad for private houses built like Greek temples (as distinct from banks and colleges). The simple masses and planes were relatively easy to execute in wooden boards and moldings, especially after the convention was adopted of substituting squared columns for round ones. The fad spread like crazy in the 1830s, spurred by the rapid settlement of the Midwest via the Erie Canal, and the Greek Revival, so called, became known also as the "National Style." Soon ordinary farmers and small-town lawyers were living in classical temples of great solemn dignity, reinforcing the association of democracy with material progress. Greek Revival houses were customarily painted white to emphasize their aura of purity. Their technical drawbacks were many, however, from inflexible floor plans to difficulty of heating.

The Greek Revival was soon superceded by another fad, for the gothic. The infatuation with things medieval was imported from England, where it signified the romantic break from eighteenth century rationalism. In America, with the slavery issue dampening our earlier transports over liberty and democracy, the gothic introduced appropriate notes of melodrama and portent. It also happened to produce more flexible, comfortable floor plans. Among the first to popularize the gothic was Alexander Jackson Davis, who had been junior partner for a while to the same Ithiel Town who had helped launch the Greek Revival. Davis, in turn, soon found an avid young partner in Andrew Jackson Downing, the Hudson Valley–based landscapist, who realized that the transportation innovations of the railroad and steamboat would open the countryside to settlement by a middle class not engaged in farming.

Meanwhile, the industrial city was giving Americans a good reason to flee to the hinterlands. The city was increasingly congested, horribly noisy, full of noxious factories, plagued by frightening epidemics such as New York's cholera outbreak in 1849, and perhaps worst of all, expanding remorselessly with no end in sight. Country living was viewed as the antidote to this frightening prospect, railroads the enabling mechanism. The paradoxes inherent in an increasingly urbanized nation yearning for rural life would only make the American Dream more piquant.

The second part of the essay, *The Beginnings of Suburbia*, continues on page 194.

Town Houses

The Carlton House in Wiscasset, Maine, built between 1804 and 1805 for Joseph Tinkham Wood, was traded to Moses Carlton, a wealthy ship owner, in 1807 for a hundred casks of rum, valued at $12,000. Wiscasset, on an expansive bay of the Sheepscot River, thirteen miles from the ocean, is blessed with one of the finest natural harbors on the coast of northern New England. The ancient forests in the vicinity of Sheepscot River provided abundant oak, spruce, and white pine for export. They also supplied timber to the local shipyards and for the houses of the merchants and shipbuilders, which, while not grand, were substantial, practical, and aesthetically pleasing. After some years of prosperity, the Revolution inflicted great hardship on the townspeople who were dependent on trade for their livelihood. After the Revolution, the townspeople industriously and success-fully labored to restore their fortunes, and the 1790s and early 1800s, when Wood built his stylish house, were the time of Wiscasset's greatest affluence. There were thriving shipyards, ropewalks, and sail lofts; and ships sailed from Wiscasset to the West Indies with lumber to trade for sugar, molasses, and rum, and to such foreign ports as Liverpool, Copenhagen, and St. Petersburg. Since Moses Carlton and his wife, Abigail, occupied the house for half a century, he became the eponym of what is still known as the Carlton house.

Opposite, right.

This façade of the Nickels-Sortwell House was built between 1807 and 1812 in Wiscasset, Maine. This, the most dazzling and extraordinary house in town, was begun for Captain William Nickels in 1807. It is three stories high with a three-story wing attached to the left rear, and, like all the grand Federal houses of the town, it has a flushboard façade. The center bay has a balustrated one-story portico supported by colonnettes of the composite order. Above the portico is a Palladian window, and, crowning the composition on the third story, a half-round, double-arched window has both radiating and oval muntins. Framing the three central bays of the upper two stories are Corinthian pilasters set above an arcaded base. If the Nickels-Sortwell house, which was completed about 1812, seems a virtual catalog of Federal architectural motifs—applied with a provincial exuberance—it must be said the result is wonderfully successful.

The parlor of the first Harrison Gray Otis House, in Boston, was-designed by Charles Bulfinch and was built in 1795 and 1796. Otis was a prototypical entrepreneur; he built on his real estate holdings in what was then called West Boston, where his first house is situated. He subsequently made a fortune developing Beacon Hill, where Bulfinch designed two further houses for him. Otis sold his house on Cambridge Street to John Osborn, a wealthy paint merchant, when he commissioned Bulfinch to build him a second house on Mt. Vernon Street in 1800. The original mantel, with its exceptionally fine neoclassical details, has recently been restored to its original appearance. The huge Boston Federal looking glass of about 1805 resembles one listed in Osborn's 1819 inventory.

The first Harrison Gray Otis House, a prime example of Federal architecture in New England, serves today as the flagship of the forty-four houses owned by the Society for the Preservation of New England Antiquities. After Osborn's death, the house passed through several owners and by the end of the nineteenth century had become a genteel rooming house in what was by then a slowly declining neighborhood. In 1916 the Cambridge Street house was bought by William Sumner Appleton to be the headquarters of the Preservation Society. In 1926 the Otis House withstood the onslaught of urban expansion; instead of being torn down to make way for the widening of Cambridge Street, it was jacked up, moved back forty feet, and attached to two adjacent town houses.

The Beacon Street area of Boston.

Boston's prosperity in the 1790s resulted in a building boom on Beacon Hill. In 1793 the commonwealth bought the pasture of John Hancock's house of 1735 as the site for the construction of the Bulfinch's State House in 1795. In the following year the Mount Vernon Proprietors began negotiations for the purchase of the twenty-acre estate of John Singleton Copley, the Boston painter and now resident of England. In 1796 this purchase was effected and the proprietors, having added by other purchases an additional nine acres to their holdings, launched their new subdivision, the largest real estate operation yet undertaken in Boston. By the century's end the proprietors had constructed an inclined wooden track on the western slope of Mount Vernon; down this track were drawn carts carrying earth from the excavation at the summit of the hill to fill the shallow tidal flats in the Charles River below. The crest of Mount Vernon was reduced about sixty feet and in 1803 Charles Street was laid out and houses rose on the new filled land. Higher up the hill, two of the proprietors built mansions for themselves—thus setting the fashion for other prosperous Boston gentlemen and establishing a high architectural standard for the neighborhood. By 1826 the proprietors' entire tract of thirty acres had been subdivided and sold except for the northwestern corner, which was laid out as Louisburg Square and its adjacent building lots. By the 1840s, practically all of the Mount Vernon subdivision was occupied.

Beacon Street in the eighteenth century ran up the hillside opposite King's Chapel beyond the property of Andrew Faneuil, a French Huguenot merchant who had settled in Boston by 1691. This handsome property, with gardens extending behind it up the hill, was inherited in 1738 by Andrew's nephew Peter Faneuil. This route led through Beacon Hill past a handful of country houses and gardens. The most remarkable of these was the three-story house built in 1722 by Edward Bromfield, behind which successive terraces, filled with flowers and fruit trees, led to a summer house which commanded a panoramic view of the harbor.

Following the excavation of Mount Vernon, Beacon Hill was the next peak to be cut down. In 1811 the Doric beacon was pulled down and the crest of Beacon Hill reduced by sixty feet. The final obliteration of Trimountain came with the drastic diminution of Cotton Hill. In 1835 the Widow Greene sold her estate, and in less than five months more than 100,000 cubic yards of gravel were hauled down the hill in oxcarts to fill the old Mill Pond (Back Bay). Fifty feet below the original crest of Cotton Hill, Pemberton Square was laid out, and building lots were auctioned off. Here, uniform, bow-front, red-brick mansions were erected, thus building over virtually all of the once-occupied land of the Tremont section. The first instance of dumping the tops of hills into coves was said by Harrison Gray Otis "to have excited as much attention as Bonaparte's road over the Alps." Boston after two hundred years was outgrowing her small peninsula, and the areas for expansion lay in the shallow flats adjacent to the neck. In this sense, Beacon Hill overflowed into the Charles Street neighborhood and onto lower Beacon Street. The town houses in these areas had swell-front façades—called also a "bow-front" or "elliptical bay."

The Market Square in Newbury, Massachusetts, with the steeple of the Church of the First Religious Society of Newburyport, built about 1801, in the background. The rise of overseas commerce from the last decades of the seventeenth into the eighteenth century wrought a profound change on the towns of eastern Massachusetts. What had begun as farming and fishing communities were gradually transformed into busy seaports. Newburyport broke off from its parent Newbury on January 28, 1764, and thereafter, the commercial interests became masters of their own houses. Now, particular groups, such as Newbury's waterside merchants and mariners, placed a higher premium on getting their own way than on preserving agreement with farmers, and took the ultimate step of secession. The establishment of a new town such as Newburyport was the result of a new concensus that embraced merchants, shipbuilders, artisans, shopkeepers, and shipwrights of varying wealth and sophistication. The third and fourth generations of Americans were discovering new and different ways of making a living. As his business expanded, the craftsman also became an employer, responsible for apprentices or hired assistants.

The Greek Revival and Opulence

Edgewater, at Barrytown, New York.

Edgewater in Barrytown, New York, was built by John Robert Livingston at about 1820 for his daughter Margaret and son-in-law Captain Lowndes Brown of Charleston, South Carolina, and was attributed on stylistic grounds to Robert Mills. The massive classical portico, with six Doric columns supporting a wide entablature decorated with triglyphs and mutules, is set in brick walls bisected by a masonry stringcourse. Robert Donaldson purchased the house in 1852, and two years later Alexander Jackson Davis designed the octagonal library at the left.

Opposite

Entrance hall of Edgewater. Margaret Livingston Brown, châtelaine of Edgewater for some thirty years, possessed not only a beautiful house but exalted family connections. Life on the banks of the Hudson, where there were such diversions as boating, picnics, balls, and amateur theatricals, must have been very pleasant. The stylish nineteenth-century geometric design was painted on the hall floor by the Canadian artist Robert Jackson in 1980.

A girandole, or convex mirror, in the library.

A French mantel clock with a likeness of George Washington.

In the drawing room at Edgewater, there are seven side chairs and a mahogany sofa attributed to Duncan Phyfe, with curule legs ending in gilded brass paws. The grand pair of girandoles or convex mirrors, surmounted by eagles and cornucopias, was made in Albany about 1815 for the De Peyster family of that city. Beneath them are a pair of neoclassical New York pier tables with stenciled decorations and marble columns that came from the Livingston family. A Swedish traveler, Frederika Bremer, who visited the Hudson River Valley in 1849 described the opulence and tranquility of life there. Of the entertainment the Donaldsons gave in her honor she commented, "The assembly was beautiful and gay, and the breakfast, which was magnificent, was closed by a dance."

In the small red sitting room off the entrance hall of Edgewater hangs a portrait of Robert Donaldson's wife Susan that was painted by George Cooke in 1832. The window seats (one of which is depicted in the painting) were made by Duncan Phyfe, possibly in 1822. The harp (which also appears in the painting) was made in London in the early nineteenth century. The bust of Washington over the door is a plaster copy of the portrait by Jean Antoine Houdon.

The octagonal addition to the library at Edgewater was designed by Alexander Jackson Davis in 1854. Davis, the younger partner of Ithiel Town, was originally trained as an artist. He emerged as one of the most significant architects of the nineteenth century by spearheading a number of influential architectural movements. The sofa in the foreground, the Grecian couch on the right, and the worktable at its head were made for Donaldson by Phyfe, probably in 1822. The armchairs flanking the fireplace and the center table are New York Empire pieces.

Millford Plantation in central South Carolina was built by Nathaniel F. Potter for John Laurence Manning and his wife, Susan Frances Hampton Manning, during the late 1830s and early 1840s. The house and its contents comprise one of the best surviving examples of the taste Americans called "Grecian" during the second quarter of the nineteenth century. Potter, a builder from Providence, Rhode Island, had been working on Hampton family projects in Charleston. Manning was the governor of South Carolina from 1852 to 1854. In the early controversies that led to the Civil War, he had been a Unionist, but after the South seceded he served the Confederacy on General Beauregard's staff. Millford's columned portico is not exclusive to the South. One finds double-height columns in front of a symmetrical block in the abolitionist North as well as the slave-holding South. Millford's portico faces northwest toward Tavern Creek and what remain of the embankments of a rice plantation.

Construction of the entrance façade began in November 1839 and was completed in May 1841. The plan of Millford follows the typical pattern of a central hall Greek Revival house; the hall is flanked on the right by a dining room with an unusual apse-shaped wall in which a central door gives access to the library. On the other side of the hall a drawing room extends the length of the house. The bases of the six Corinthian columns were specified by the builder Potter as Rhode Island granite, and they may have been delivered already shaped. The column shafts were constructed of bricks made on the site with a machine bought by the owner John Laurence Manning. The flutes of the columns were fashioned with stucco, and the elaborate acanthus leaves and tendrils were carved from pine. Iron summer beams spanned the columns, supporting bricks that were plastered to form the entablature that encircles the house. The exterior walls were also of brick covered with stucco.

The main entrance of Millford Plantation is flanked by Corinthian columns and framed by two smaller columns confined between square piers, or antae. In the mid 1830s, the ebullient character of Corinthian architecture offered a contrast to the plain and severe Doric style of American Grecian architecture. The Grecian style is found in the monumental Corinthian columns on the front of the house, where the capitals are patterned after those on the Choragic Monument of Lysicrates in Athens. The unknown architect of that small structure, built in 334 BCE, was the first to use Corinthian columns on an exterior. The Lysicrates type of Corinthian capital was revived in the United States with the publication of Minard Lafever's *Beauties of Modern Architecture* in 1935. His book was in turn based on the exquisite engravings of the Choragic Monument of Lysicrates in the first volume of Stuart and Revett's immensely influential *Antiquities of Athens*, first published in London in 1762. The builder, Nathaniel F. Potter, specified a "Colonnade to be composed of six Corinthian columns, the style to be used is that from the monument of Lysicratus."

In the dining room are a number of armchairs with gondola backs that were delivered to Millford by Phyfe and Son: some of the surviving armchairs are mahogany and others are rosewood. Their design is based on that of chairs made in Paris in the Restauration style, which, in turn, is a variation of the Napoleonic Empire style simplified for a bourgeois clientele. Whereas the chairs in the drawing room are decorated with some carved elements, the set of fourteen chairs in the dining room, based on the same pattern, are not carved. Their lower cost reflects the somewhat humbler status of the dining room—a hierarchy maintained in the frames on the overmantel mirrors in the two rooms. The remarkably harmonious environment of the restored Manning's house and its original furnishings expands our understanding of American culture in the genteel South before the Civil War.

John Manning was born in 1816 at Hickory Hill Plantation in Clarendon County, South Carolina. His father, Richard Irvine Manning, was the governor of South Carolina between 1824 and 1826, and his mother, Elizabeth Peyre Richardson Manning, was

the sister, niece, mother, and grandmother of other governors of South Carolina. Young John Manning attended Princeton University, where he was so impressed at how the winter cold was relieved by basement furnaces that he later had one installed in Millford.

Opposite

Millford's cylindrical stair hall is lit by this window and a stained-glass oculus in a shallow dome. Around the oculus are plaster rosettes in imitation of ancient Greek patterns. The stair is not located within the central hall, as is typically the case in most Greek Revival houses, but is housed in a cylinder grafted onto the back of the house. At the base of the stair a pair of doors opens onto a piazza sheltered by a roof that extends laterally at both sides to form covered walkways to the cubic kitchen and laundry pavilions. As built, Millford's abstract juxtaposition of the cylinder and boxlike dependencies presents a startling geometry in architectural appearance.

The long drawing room at Millford is visually divided by a quartet of Corinthian columns that support the bedroom walls on the second floor, and it can actually be separated into two rooms with mirrored partitions that fold out from the side walls. Befitting the standards of the day, Millford's drawing room was the important interior, richly decorated with Grecian motifs in plaster. Ample illumination is provided by eight large, double-hung windows; the front and rear windows extend to the floor "so as to allow a person to pass under without obstruction." Manning's family papers include letters and a bill of lading from Duncan Phyfe and Son of New York City. In 1841 and 1842 the famous firm delivered an enormous quantity of furniture to Manning's factory in Charleston, South Carolina. The builder Potter's specifications for Millford are peppered with references and allusions to Minard Lafever's *Beauties of Modern Architecture* (1835). He made three direct references to Lafever's book. The "sliding and folding doors" in the drawing room are based on Plate 7, the majority of the door and window casings are based on Plate 19, and the interior decoration of the main doorway is based on Plate 13. Other plates from Lafever were used but not specified. The plaster ceiling rosettes in the drawing room, for example, are found in Plate 21, and the many Lysicrates capitals are based on Plate 43.

Preceding page: The ballroom at Nottoway

Opposite, right
The stairway of Poplar Hall,
near Dover, Delaware, was
rebuilt in 1804 after a fire.
The clock, made locally,
and the English mezzotints
hanging on the wall date from
the eighteenth century.

A Gatefold of Early-Nineteenth-Century Stairways, Doorways, and Façades

Opposite, right
The stairway of Poplar Hall,
near Dover, Delaware, was
rebuilt in 1804 after a fire.
The clock, made locally,
and the English mezzotints
hanging on the wall date from
the eighteenth century.

Nottoway sits about 200 feet behind the Mississippi levee surrounded by oaks, magnolias, pecan trees, and sweet olives. From the front gallery the river is in view.

This enormous mansion, completed in 1859, reflects an unusual combination. Nottoway is distinctive for being an essentially Italianate-style plantation house built in an era dominated by Greek Revival architecture. Nottoway contains an elegant, half-round portico as the side gallery follows the curve of the large ballroom bay window. Nottoway's thin Italianate pillars stretch vertically to touch all of its three levels, extending from the house's one-story brick base to the paramount height of the third story, which has a wooden frame. The architectural elements blend with the fanciful desires of the original owner. Not only is the floor plan irregular, but the house contained many elements that were innovative and rare in the mid-nineteenth century, such as indoor plumbing and hot and cold running water.

Nottoway survived the Civil War. Some damage occurred when a Union gunboat on the Mississippi River attempted to destroy the magnificent house but the gunboat officer realized he had once been a guest there and decided to spare the home.

The expertly carved window surrounds in the parlor of the Lee-Payson-Smith house in Wiscasset, built for Judge Silas Lee in 1792. This well-designed arch with elaborate Ionic pilasters framing the parlor window recalls the window treatments in Federal houses in Newburyport and Portsmouth.

The door of the 1800 Joseph Wilson house in Newburyport, Massachusetts, is framed by two Corinthian-style fluted pilasters and a simple elliptical fanlight.

The Greek Revival doorway of the 1834 John Marlor House
in Milledgeville, Georgia.

The transom above the double doors at Hancock Shaker Village is an example of "borrowed light." The innovative Shakers frequently installed windows inside their buildings, between small rooms, near stairways, and in attics.

Left and above
Named for a seventeenth-century beacon that stood just behind the State House's current location, Beacon Hill is all that remains of Tremontaine, the distinctive three-peaked hill that gave Tremont Street its name. The South Slope started to be developed in the 1790s with homes for some of the wealthiest and most influential families in Boston. The mansions and townhouses housed a community of philosophers, writers, and philanthropists ranging from Oliver Wendell Holmes to Henry Wadsworth Longfellow to Louisa May Alcott.

Approximately one mile square, Beacon Hill is bounded by Beacon Street, Bowdoin Street, Cambridge Street, and Storrow Drive. It is known for its beautiful doors, decorative iron work, brick sidewalks, gas lights, flowering pear trees, window boxes, and hidden gardens. Its architecture, mostly brick row houses, includes the Federal, Greek Revival, and Victorian periods, as well as early twentieth-century Colonial revival homes and tenements. The area is protected by regulations that allow no changes to any visible part of a structure without the approval of an architectural commission.

The spectacular flying staircase of the Federal Style Ruggles House, in Columbia Falls, Maine. Thomas Ruggles was a timber exporter and shipowner who began to build this house in 1818 and completed it in 1820.

Ruggles hired two craftsmen from afar to create the sophisticated design and details never before seen in this part of northern Maine. They worked with finesse, overlaying imported mahogany, fluting, carving, and turning in true virtuoso style. Sadly, Ruggles died at the end of the year the house was completed.

The dining room at Nottaway, Louisiana, frequently used for entertaining, was the most elegant room in the house. It contained every-day objects and pieces "for show." Breakfast and dinner, a meal normally served in the early afternoon, were usually eaten there. Because travel was difficult and often involved great distances, guests usually stayed awhile. "Southern hospitality" evolved from these visits. Due to the large families and frequent visitors, big tables were necessary. When fully extended, they could seat twelve to fourteen people. Inexpensive Chinese porcelains were found in up-country homes by 1860. The cost, as well as the possibility of breakage during shipment from the North, meant a family valued its glassware. By the 1850s many up-country families used silver for dining. This flatware, made in South Carolina, was cheaper than the more highly prized Northern or European silver, and new planters often showed off by using it.

The French Influence

The Henri Penne House in Iberia Parish, Louisiana, was built between about 1821 and 1830 and was moved in 1974 twenty miles to the Anse La Butte ("cove on the hill") district near the town of Breaux Bridge in Saint Martin Parish, Louisiana, and there was faithfully restored. In the new location, as in the old, the front yard is encircled by live oaks. The fenced parterre garden is based in part on a nearby garden planted about 1835. In addition to the Penne house, the Petite Maison, a pigeonnier, a storage building, two privies, and a period garden are arranged to recreate a fairly complete Creole plantation. The Penne house originally faced El Camino Real, the old Spanish trail on the west side of the present town of Jeanerette in Iberia Parish. One would expect a Louisiana house of this period built for a French-born citizen to reflect many French Colonial influences, but there are really only two: that the principal rooms open directly onto the front galleries and that an exterior staircase leads from the gallery to the half story. The Henri Penne house exhibits far more Anglo-American characteristics. Its central hall is flanked by two rooms on either side; the six-panel double entrance doors have side lights and a glazed transom; and the clapboarded brick-between-posts structure has a gable-end roof and double-hung sash windows.

The salon of the Henri Penne house is furnished with French furniture in the Louis Philippe style and American examples from the late Federal and Empire period. The Penne house was built for Henri Marie Penne Sr., who was born in Nantes, France, in 1767, and died in Charenton, Louisiana, in 1847. The house was erected between about 1821 and 1830 on land that Penne's wife had inherited in 1812. The date for the construction of the residence is predicated in part on Penne's sale of two pieces of property in 1821, which would have provided him the money to build his Federal style house. The Louisiana soil on both sides of the Mississippi below the mouth of the Red River was ideal for cotton planting, but most of South Louisiana was sugar country. While the great planters did dominate the countryside, most Louisiana farmers were yeomen who engaged primarily in subsistence agriculture. They planted some cotton, and occasionally, in the southern part of the state, some sugar as a source of cash, but basically they concentrated on growing the corn and livestock upon which their families lived. Corn was the basic food for man and beast in Louisiana, and the growing of corn was essential to the production of cotton and sugar. "Everything eats corn from slave to chick," the English novelist-economist Harriet Martineau complained of the American South in 1837.

In the dining room of the Penne House, the mahogany and oak dining table was made in France, about 1830 to 1845, but was found in New Iberia, Louisiana. The fourteen American mahogany fiddle-back chairs of about 1835 are an assembled set of a type that was popular in Louisiana. The table is set with vieux Paris porcelain collected locally. The pelmets over the windows are made of antique French silk and cotton fabric. The Penne house is furnished with a combination of American Federal and Empire furniture and Louisiana Creole and Acadian furniture made between 1750 and 1835.

This Acadian bedroom of the Penne House features a low-post bed of 1830 to 1840 that is from Saint Landry Parish, Louisiana, and that reflects the blending of Anglo-American and French Louisiana characteristics. The basic style is Anglo American, but the poles supporting mosquito nets and the use of swamp maple, ash, and cypress for the woods are Acadian. The Acadian quilt on the bed was woven from white, indigo-dyed, and natural yellow cotton threads in different and fairly complex patterns. The pine and birch cradle at the foot of the bed is French Canadian but was found in Baton Rouge. In the foreground is a copy of Volume II of Denis Diderot's *Encyclopédie* (1772) with illustrations and the tools needed for weaving. Between 1765 and 1785 the Acadians moved into Louisiana's Mississippi River Delta marshlands.

Exiled after French Acadia became English Nova Scotia, they isolated themselves to reestablish their society along the bayous and on the prairies. There they built small line villages according to a system of community organization and land division that had begun to mature in French Canada. By the nineteenth century, the varied French cultures, enriched by Native American tribes and immigrants from Germany, Spain, Italy, Ireland, and England, created a people who came to be called "Cajun." In south Louisiana a pronounced French influence continues. In addition to Catholicism and to French, which is spoken today by about 373,500 Cajuns, they maintain an architectural tradition of a four-room, story-and-a-half frame cottage with a narrow incorporated front porch.

Christmas Celebration

The Van Cortlandt Manor in Croton-on-Hudson, New York, built in the late seventeenth century and remodeled in 1749 by Pierre Van Cortlandt I. The house is furnished largely with objects that belonged to the Van Cortlandt family and were used during their 250-year occupancy, which stretched from the late seventeenth century through the early years of the twentieth century. The manor house and outbuildings were the center of a vast estate devoted to farming, milling, and trade. The Van Cortlandts were patriots during the Revolution, and this accounts for the survival of the family furnishings. While most large landholders wanted a national government strong enough to protect property rights and therefore endorsed the Federalist position, Pierre Van Cortlandt was one of the few who were numbered among the Anti-Federalists.

Opposite, right

From the ceiling in the entrance hall of the Van Cortlandt Manor in Croton-on-Hudson hangs a kissing bell used by celebrants of Christmas "old style" on January 6. The portrait of Abraham Van Cortlandt is attributed to Gerardus Duyckinck I or Evert Duyckinck III and was painted about 1727. Many of the early settlers of the Hudson River Valley in New York were Dutch Protestants and Huguenots who brought with them the manners and customs of the European lowlands. Then, in 1664, the English seized New Netherlands and infused the colony with new traditions. Many of the Dutch and Huguenots converted to the Anglican religion. Dutch as a language persisted in certain areas well into the nineteenth century and the text of prayer books was often printed both in English and Dutch. The Dutch in New York, having adopted the Gregorian calendar, celebrated Christmas on December 25. The English began using the Gregorian calendar in 1751, but apparently the earlier Julian calendar prevailed for years afterwards in some places. The Julian calendar, which lagged behind the Gregorian by eleven days, put Christmas on January 6, coinciding with Epiphany, on Twelfth Night, as celebrated by those using the Gregorian calendar. Thus Pierre Van Cortlandt II wrote his son on January 6, 1836: "Yesterday was Christmas [eve] old stile (N. Year old style will be Thursday next). This tradition your grandfather observed all his life."

Mantel shelf in the parlor of Van Cortlandt Manor. The early nineteenth-century French shelf clock was sold to Major General Pierre Van Cortlandt in 1809 by N. Taylor and Company of New York City. Lemons used as Christmas decorations reflected the value of citrus fruit at that time of year.

126

Sunnyside, the home of Washington Irving, stands on the banks of the Hudson River in Tarrytown, New York. The estate possessed a unique allure for its creator, and offers an intimate glance at his interests and achievements. Writer, intellectual, diplomat, antiquarian, and an American hero celebrated on both sides of the Atlantic, Washington Irving designed Sunnyside as a retreat at the end of his glorious career. The structure, more than a literary shrine to the First American Man of Letters, serves as a quintessential symbol of the era in American history that produced it. The house is composed of a mixture of historical styles chosen to give the effect of great age. Nestled into a lush, slightly wild landscape, Sunnyside epitomizes the then-prevalent Romantic movement in architecture and landscape design, expressive of a yearning for an idealized past. Sunnyside's melange of styles represents Irving's many interests, including a fascination with Dutch, Scottish, and Spanish history. The stepped parapet gables that Irving added to the cottage between 1835 and 1837 are reminiscent of the Dutch-influenced urban architecture of early Manhattan. The result, in Irving's own words, is "a little, old-fashioned stone mansion all made up of gabled ends, and as full of angles and corners as an old cocked hat." Stepped gables are also part of Scotland's grammar of ornament and, as such, are found on the home of Sir Walter Scott, a man whom Irving admired personally and professionally.

The dining room of Sunnyside on the west side of the house offers a handsome river view. Here Irving, his family, and guests took their main meal, consisting of several courses as was the custom, at three o'clock. An air of hospitality pervaded Sunnyside, and Irving's impressive guest list included Charles Louis Napoleon Bonaparte (later Napoleon III), Dr. Oliver Wendell Holmes, and Martin Van Buren. Irving made the dining room all the more inviting by decorating it with portraits of family friends and comfortable furniture. One visitor remarked upon dining at Sunnyside with the Baltimore novelist John Pendleton Kennedy: "We had two 'Mr. Kennedys' in the dining room . . . our friend's portrait, as he sat at the dining-table, hanging directly over his head." Irving family possessions include a brass and cut-glass chandelier, Gothic Revival dining chairs, and a French porcelain dessert service, which, according to family tradition, belonged to Sarah Paris Storrow, a favorite niece of Irving's.

Washington Irving observed Christmas at Sunnyside on December 25 each year, often surrounded by members of his family. His letters abound in references to Christmas, when Sunnyside was decked in greens in the manner of an English country house, such as the one Irving described in *Bracebridge Hall* (1822). He wrote from Sunnyside to his niece Sara Paris Storrow on January 25, 1854: "Our Christmas holidays passed off with quiet enjoyment. There was as usual a gathering of part of the family at the cottage. The little mansion as usual was decked with Christmas greens, and when the party broke up and returned to town they all professed to have passed a very merry Christmas."

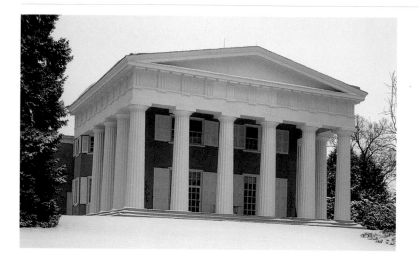

The east front of Andalusia on the Delaware River in Andalusia, Pennsylvania, located halfway between Pennsbury and Philadelphia. Built as a summerhouse in 1797 and 1798 for John and Margaret Murphy Craig; enlarged by Benjamin Henry Latrobe as the mansion Andalusia between 1806 and 1808; and again between 1834 and 1836 after his daughter Jane married Nicholas Biddle. After Biddle wanted to expand the Craig villa to reflect his rising position and economic success as president of the Second Bank of the United States, he invited the young architect Thomas Ustick Walter, whose revised design for Girard College Biddle had already supervised as chairman of the trustees. Walter, a native Philadelphian, had been trained by William Stickland. Eventually he would become the dean of mid-nineteenth century American architects and a founder of the American Institute of Architects. In the 1850s, he would cap his career by designing the wings and dome of the United States Capitol, arguably the most identifiable building in the country. Andalusia would be his most famous residential commission. Biddle and Walter considered making the house into a miniature Parthenon, with a single row of columns around the perimeter and with eight across the pedimented ends. Walter, however, favored a simpler and less expensive hexastyle structure (six columns across) based on the surviving fifth-century BCE Doric-style Temple of Theseum in Athens. Only Biddle had actually seen these temples, but Walter owned the seminal book of American neoclassicism, James Stuart and Nicholas Revett's *Antiquities of Athens*.

The yellow parlor at Andalusia shown on the right contains objects acquired over several generations of Biddles. The room was remodeled by Walter. The Italian marble mantel and white and gilt overmantel mirror were ordered especially for the house in the 1830s by Biddle. Acting as agent for his parents, Edward Craig Biddle acquired the chandelier from the Paris firm of Thomire & Cie in 1836. The maple sofa table with a painted slate top carries the label of Anthony G. Querville, a Philadelphia cabinetmaker of the 1820s and 1830s.

Farmhouses and Frontier Culture

The Homeplace 1850, part of the Land Between the Lakes open-air museum on the Tennessee-Kentucky border, recalls the life of a farm family between the Tennessee and Cumberland rivers, in the mid-nineteenth century. The double-crib house shown on the preceeding page was built by the Bussell family before 1845. A crib is a space enclosed by stacking logs in layers or courses at right angles to the layer immediately below. The double-crib houses consist of two spaces enclosed by stacked logs and covered by a common roof. This front view shows the open hall or "dog trot" that joins the two cribs or "pens" on either side. The dog trot was favored in the South because it made an airy, cooler place for the family to eat or do chores in warm weather. The family could also enjoy resting on the full-length porches on the front and back of the house. There are five rooms altogether: a main front room (where the family dined and the parents slept), a parlor, a girls' room, a boys' room, and a kitchen addition in a separate crib on the back of the main house.

On the right is a back view of Homeplace farmhouse, showing the main log house with the kitchen addition on the right. The roof extends over an open space between the main house and the kitchen, creating an open hall area in the back porch that runs the length of the building. The construction of the kitchen addition is typical of the region, with log walls and clapboard gables.

The kitchen of the Homeplace is furnished with a cast-iron cookstove, which brought the business of cooking off the floor of the hearth to a more comfortable waist height. John Conant, a Vermont investor, patented an iron cooking stove in 1819 that created a revolution in cooking equipment. Until then, most cooking had been done over an open fire at the hearth or in a primitive enclosed brick oven heated with coals that had to be raked out before cooking could begin. The solid-fuel iron range came into general use in middle-class homes in the 1860s, and the gas version twenty years later. (Gas ovens had in fact been used in London's Reform Club as early as 1838, but people remained suspicious of gas, especially of its smell, for some time.)

As early as 1795, however, the émigré physician Benjamin Thompson, born in Massachusetts and known as Count Rumford, had invented a stove that was economical on fuel. He developed a closed-top range that provided adjustable heat from a small fire controlled by a battery of flues, blowpipes, dampers, and metal plates. Thompson abandoned his wife and daughter at Concord after the outbreak of the American Revolution and recieved his title in 1791 from the elector of Bavaria. He demonstrated with the Rumford oven that 1,200 of the poor of Munich could be fed on barley soup, thickened with potatoes and bread and seasoned with vinegar, at a cost of half-a-penny each per day, but the poor resisted the idea of eating potatoes.

The Farmhouse at the Mountain Farm Museum in North Carolina was built in 1901 by John E. Davis, a master craftsman who took the trouble to "match" the log walls—he split a chestnut tree trunk in half, then used matching logs to construct each wall. Davis was also an itinerant cooper who made and sold barrels, buckets, and churns, and he made furniture. Davis moved to this area in the 1880s as a renter, eventually marrying and buying land of his own. He built the farmhouse over two years in his spare time from trees cleared from the house site. His reasons for building with logs over readily available timber from sawmills may have included his desire to use trees cleared from the site and to do the work at his own convenience.

The great middle class, whose presence generally gave North Carolina its distinctive character, was dominated by those who owned smaller tracts of land, which they farmed themselves. Every settler who undertook to clear land on the frontier in the backcountry and build a home for his family did so on an equal footing with his neighbor, although there were a few newcomers who had the advantage of some extra money to spend on livestock and tools. Soon the men with greater incentive, drive, and capability emerged from the masses and laid the foundation for social, economic, and political variety. Clever and thrifty men found it possible to buy additional .land from lazy neighbors and from those who could not resist the temptation of chasing the frontier and moving farther west. With this growth came the other members of the middle class, the skilled artisans, traders, clerks, and various assistants to the professional classes.

The house is raised on stone piers and does not have a cellar. The rocky soil in this region made digging root cellars hard work, so some families dug an opening into a hillside and finished it with a roof and door to serve as a "tater cave." The Davis sons helped their father by collecting stones for the chimney with an ox-drawn sled. While fieldstone chimneys were typically dry-laid without mortar, mud, when used, served merely as daubing to fill in the chinks between stones to improve the chimney's draft. The social customs of the people of the North Carolina backcountry were not much different from those prevailing in the other colonies. Early and frequent marriages, for example, were common. Land and raw materials were plentiful and relatively easy to acquire, but it was lonely for a man on the frontier. A woman was needed for her companionship as well as her ability to perform the chores required by the various household industries. If a farm was to achieve self-sufficiency, a woman and children were virtually impossible to do without. Women married young and large families were the rule, the average number of children being five to seven. The inscriptions on tombstones in burying grounds are silent witness to the fact that women, far more than men, typically died young. It was not often that a woman had a second husband, but there were few men who failed to marry a second time; many, in fact, married a third and some even a fourth time.

In the 1950s, the builder, John Davis, recalled he did not use mud daubing, which required annual maintenance because it dried out, was bored into by insects, and was washed away in hard rains. Instead he used rived boards, or long pieces of wedge-shaped wood, like long shingles, inserting them into the chinks. In the late eighteenth century, the Scotch Irish came flooding down from Pennsylvania along the Great Wagon Road, settling the Valley of Virginia's southern end and moving into the backcountry of North Carolina. Of the pioneers who settled the piedmont and river valleys of North Carolina, about one-third were Scotch-Irish families. Undisciplined, emotional, courageous, aggressive, pugnacious, fiercely intolerant, and hard-drinking, with a tendency to indolence, they nevertheless produced ambitious leaders with the virtues of the warrior and politician. The Scotch Irish came into North Carolina in great numbers only after Pennsylvania, Maryland, and Virginia no longer offered suitable land at a price they could afford to pay. The Scotch Irish in North Carolina became good substantial farmers, seldom planters. About seventy-five percent of them had farms of between one hundred and five hundred acres; five percent had fewer than one hundred acres; and five percent held over a thousand acres.

The log cabin is a symbol of the hardships and virtues of simple life, integrity, and democratic values. Many noted Americans, including five presidents—Andrew Jackson, James Polk, James Buchanan, Abraham Lincoln, and James Garfield— proudly claimed they were born in such dwellings. Log houses were unknown to Native Americans, and without the benefit of archaeological research, popular opinion in the nineteenth century was that the early seventeenth-century English colonists must have put up the first log homes.

People in Europe had been building log cabins for hundreds of years before Europeans came to America. It is a generally accepted hypothesis that log cabins were introduced in America by Swedish settlers in the Delaware Valley in 1638. Log cabin construction spread to many other groups of colonists, including English, Welsh, and Dutch settlers. Eventually, log cabin construction could be found throughout the wooded American frontier. Even the Scotch-Irish, who did not possess a log-building tradition of their own, adapted the form of the stone houses of their native country to log construction, and contributed to spreading it across the frontier. By the end of the eighteenth century the log house was the typical backwoods dwelling. It was universally used by settlers in the West until they reached the Great Plains, where the sod house was the customary dwelling. Reappearing in the Rockies, the log cabin was the perfect pioneer dwelling. Much of frontier America was a vast forest, and the log cabin could be quickly built with nothing more than an axe.

The simplest log cabins were built of round logs with curved notches cut near the ends. Logs on the ground served as a foundation. Above the foundation, each log lay across the logs immediately below it and rested in their notches. In most cases, spaces between the logs were filled with stones or slats of wood and daubed tight with mud in a process called "chinking." The roof was usually made of rough boards cut from logs.

Most Americans left their log cabin for a better dwelling as soon as possible, but it was still able to capture the imagination of the American people. Political supporters of 1840 presidential candidate William Henry Harrison appropriated the log cabin as a campaign symbol when supporters of his Democratic opponent, Martin Van Buren, said that he lived in a log cabin and drank hard cider. In a circus-like and acrimonious campaign, the Whigs turned these remarks against the Democrats. They were proud to paint their own aristocratic Harrison now as a log-cabin-dwelling, hard-cider-drinking frontiersman who was a major military hero; Van Buren was labeled as a champagne-sipping dandy and plutocrat. Coonskin caps, miniature log cabins, and plenty of hard cider appeared at Whig rallies. Log cabins just like the one illustrated here were even used as campaign headquarters.

Eventually log building was phased out by balloon frame construction. However, later in the century, log construction was employed in new ways. In the 1870s, wealthy Americans initiated the Great Camp Movement for rustic vacation retreats in the Adirondack Mountains of upstate New York. Developers such as William Durant, used natural materials, including wood shingles, stone, and log— often with its bark retained to emphasize the rustic style—designed comfortable summer houses and lodges that blended with the natural setting.

This Valley of Virginia nineteenth-century farm at the Museum of American Frontier Culture features a log house, a double-pen cantilevered log barn, and a tobacco barn, all typical of western Virginia architecture. The farmstead reflects a blending of architectural traditions from Germany and the British Isles. The original section of the two-story log house, to the left of the chimney, was built in the 1830s. The rectangular house plan, with one room on each floor, an end chimney, and a central front door, reflected building traditions from Ireland and England. Oak roof singles are the primary roofing material, although tin roofing, introduced to the area in the mid-nineteenth century, is used on the root cellar. In the 1840s, the kitchen–pantry with a root cellar underneath was added. At that time, the entire house was sheathed with weatherboards and the front and back porches were added.

The Valley of Virginia farmhouse's kitchen table is set for a family meal; the staircase above leads to an unfinished pantry. The interior of the log house features exposed whitewashed log walls, beaded ceiling joists, a molded chair rail, and enclosed corner stairwells. Hanging on racks against the whitewashed wall is part of the harvest from the farm's orchard and kitchen garden. Carefully sliced and dried green beans, tomatoes, peppers, apples, squash, and pumpkin wait to be reconstituted by being soaked in water for winter meals.

The Great Valley of Virginia became a melting pot of national and international styles in the decorative arts. English furniture forms were adopted by German artisans and decorated in regional styles from a number of German states. Backcountry potters fashioned earthenware in the Staffordshire style, adding urban elements to ancient traditions of colorful slip-decorated peasant wares. Backcountry furnaces offered cast iron in any style preferred by their customers.

The log kitchen wing of the Valley of Virginia farmstead was added to the original farmhouse in the 1840s, considerably improving the comfort and convenience of the home. The fireplace and the extended hearth area were used for open-hearth cooking; the family dined in the kitchen as well. Whitewashing the walls, an annual housekeeping task, brightened and sanitized the room. The floor covering is a painted floor cloth, a sturdy piece of canvas decorated with oil paint. The resulting handiwork was an attractive, durable, washable surface that was the ancestor of today's linoleum and vinyl flooring.

Pierced with numerous passes all along its length, the Valley of Virginia served as a highway in the eighteenth century, as settlers moved along its floor in search of new land. By the middle of the eighteenth-century, with this steady flow of immigrants from Pennsylvania filling up the valley, Virginians were eyeing the country beyond the Alleghenies. A correspondent in Kentucky wrote in 1786 that "it will be as practicable to turn a torrent of water backward, as to prevent the amazing emigration to this country . . . they are of all nations, tongues and languages, from our own country, and every part of Europe they are gathered."

The Kvalle farmhouse, built in 1848 in Wisconsin, reflects traditional log-building techniques that characterized Norwegian-American settlement. Now part of the Old World Wisconsin open-air museum, the house built by Anders Kvalle shares the plan of almost all of the early houses constructed by Norwegian immigrants, with three rooms of unequal size on both the ground and second floors and a long gallery, or *sval*, running the length of the second floor, above the porch. When it was built, the porch of this farmhouse was open along the length of the house, but as the family grew, more space was necessary, and a portion of the porch was walled in and permanently converted to a living area. In the early 1840s, Wisconsin began to attract many Norwegian immigrants, who were more likely than not to settle in the countryside and farm. By the time this house was built, the immigrants were borrowing some American construction methods, such as the lapped siding of the second-floor gable and the neat, squared-off corners of the logs.

The bedroom shown on the left in the Ketola family farmhouse opens into the kitchen; the house was built in stages from 1894 to 1900 in Bayfield County, Wisconsin, and is an excellent example of Finnish log construction. Patchwork quilts, such as the one covering the bed, were made in the farm wife's spare time and were the only warm coverings available for the long winter months. At the time that Wisconsin became the thirtieth state, in 1848, Americans and Europeans were swarming westward in search of cheap land and an opportunity to start life anew. Wisconsin welcomed the home-seekers, both native and foreign-born. The 1860 census showed that Wisconsin, in proportion to its population, contained more immigrants than any other state except California. In the 1870s and 1880s Wisconsin continued to receive a large share of immigrants, particularly Germans and Scandinavians.

144

The Model Farmhouse

Living History Farms in Urbandale, Iowa, includes this accurately restored turn-of-the-century progressive farm. The complex, which includes a modest farmhouse, barn, stable, and several smaller out-buildings, evidences the social and technological changes of the progressive farm movement. American agriculture was being trans-formed from small, labor-intensive, but self-sufficient farms to larger, more efficient, and less personal operations.

It was the black soil that brought the early settlers into Iowa and distributed them evenly across its broad valley. The rich premium land was here, only men and machines were needed to turn it into a garden. Of the 56,000 square miles contained within the state's boundaries, ninety-eight percent is now under cultivation, the largest percentage of any state in the nation. Agriculture has always been the omniculture of the state. Iowa alone of all the midwestern states east of the Missouri River has no central metropolitan area to dominate the state's social, economic,

and political structure. Its largest city, Des Moines, with only slightly more than 200,000 people, does not rank in population among the top one hundred cities of the nation, and its next largest city, Cedar Rapids, is only half the size of Des Moines. Iowa has remained the state with the largest number of farm residents, both in percentage and in absolute numbers, of any state in the country.

Late-nineteenth-century farmhouses combined elements from many sources—local building traditions, nationally distributed pattern books, and the considerable output of the agricultural press. While many houses influenced by these varied materials looked like mongrel breeds, with Victorian, Gothic, and eclectic details, the progressive farmhouse, like this one in Urbandale, Iowa, was free of fancy, a simple white clapboard structure that took pride in its efficiency, rather than its flamboyance.

Once the land was cleared, the Iowa farmer's concerns were the eternal problems of the tillers of the soil: weather, infestation of pests, plant disease, fencing, transportation of his crops to market, and current market prices. During much of the nineteenth century, the Iowa farmer was blessed with good weather conditions—adequate rainfall and long growing seasons. But with the turning of the first prairie sod, the ecological balance that nature had achieved in the grasslands was forever disturbed. The prairie grasses, which had grown resistant to plant diseases, were plowed under. The imported cultivated plants—wheat, oats, flax, and fruit trees—alien to the land, were only too vulnerable to disease. With thousands of acres under cultivation, the fungi of rust, scab, and orchard blight moved in on their rich feast; so too came the grasshoppers in great clouds, like the biblical plagues of Egypt. Only Indian maize or corn, perhaps because it had for so long been cultivated by Native Americans, appeared resistant to the diseases. By the 1880s, the Iowa farmer had turned mainly to corn. Iowa had found its true destiny as corn raiser and hog producer for the nation.

145

The Firestone Farm was built in 1828 in Columbiana County, Ohio, the birthplace of Harvey S. Firestone, the American businessman and rubber baron of automobile tire fame. The farmhouse and outbuildings were moved to Greenfield Village in Dearborn, Michigan, and opened to the public as a restored, working farm in 1985. Henry Ford and Harvey Firestone were close friends and fellow members of a small group of kindred spirits who humorously called themselves the "vagabonds" (other members were Thomas Edison and the naturalist John Burroughs). When it was constructed in 1828, the Firestone farmhouse was a traditional four-over-four Pennsylvania-German house, with four upstairs rooms over four downstairs rooms. The double front doors are the distinctive feature of the exterior. The rooms on the first floor had mixed public and private uses: the *kuche*, a large kitchen that also served as a casual eating area; the *stube*, a more formal living room, dining room, and parlor; and the *kammer*, a sitting room or bedroom in the back of the house. Four interconnected bedrooms on the second floor opened into each other in a way that did not allow for privacy. The interior of the house featured exposed wooden ceiling joists and wooden board walls painted in bright, chalky colors. The Firestones remodeled the house extensively in 1882, eliminating the vestiges of its humble Pennsylvania-German origins and providing it with a modern appearance, from the ornamental front porch and roof slates to stylish wallpaper and dropped ceilings inside.

The main kitchen of the 1900 farm in Urbandale, Iowa, has a large, up-to-date cast-iron cookstove, with plenty of burners and an energy-efficient oven door. On the oil-cloth-covered table is a potato ricer, another labor-saving device introduced during this period; the kitchen also has an early screen door, a space-saving rack for drying towels over the cookstove, and a mail-ordered chair in the corner.

Women played a very large role in the development of the progressive farm. The major agricultural periodicals, such as the *American Agriculturalist*, the *Ohio Farmer*, and the *American Farmer*, published house and farm plans and helpful household tips provided by their readers, and women contributed a great number of farmhouse designs. In addition to the general layout of the house, farm wives focused on the kitchen, necessarily the room where they spent most of their working hours. In this 1900 farmhouse, the kitchen has been split in two; there is a main kitchen with the stove, and the back kitchen pictured here, where baked goods and some supplies were stored. On the right-hand side wall is a Hoosier cabinet with a built-in flour dispenser, and at the back is a pie safe topped with several kerosene lanterns. The small saucers beneath the pie safe's legs are practically filled with water, preventing ants from reaching the baked goods inside the safe. The tin panels are punched in a decorative pattern with a small awl to allow ventilation without admitting flying insects. In this part of Iowa, the sharp edges of the holes project outward, providing a greater deterrent against insects. Mason's reusable screw-cap jars for canning freed farm families from having to rely on pickle barrels, root cellars, and smokehouses to get through the winter. Urban families used Mason jars as well, to put up excess fruits and vegetables, especially tomatoes, sweet corn, berries, peaches, relish, and pickles. Ball-Mason jars were introduced by Ball Brothers Glass Manufacturing Company of Muncie, Indiana, in 1887.

His method of boiling meat and vegetables in jars, then sealing them with corks and tar, which had taken fourteen years to perfect, would remain briefly a French military secret. Then in 1858, John Landis Mason, a twenty-six-year-old New York metalworker, patented a glass container with a thread molded into its top and a zinc lid with a threaded ring sealer—the Mason jar.

Conserving and Preserving

The pantry of Cobblestone Farm in Ann Arbor, Michigan, was built in 1844 by Dr. Benjamin Ticknor, a U.S. Navy surgeon. The built-in cupboard provided storage preserves in the upper section, over bins for flour and sugar below. The crocks and glass jars are characteristic containers for the period. The tray-like object on the bottom shelf is a butter worker, used to remove all traces of buttermilk from newly churned butter. The wooden item on the shelf above is a slaw cutter, or encased blade for efficiently slicing cabbage into sauerkraut. Until the early nineteenth century, most of the known preservation techniques for food had been in use for at least 2,000 years. But by the seventeenth century, good housewives in Europe had gained the knowledge of how to conserve cooked meats for a limited time by covering them with a thick layer of fat, which excluded air. A hundred years later women were putting their fruit syrups and conserves in "viall glasses," and by 1804 Nicolas Appert opened the world's first vacuum-bottling factory, or cannery, packing food for Napoleon's armies.

The pantry off the kitchen in the Kelley Farmhouse, in Elk River, Minnesota, and built for Oliver Kelley in 1876, has a cupboard for storing dry goods—flour, sugar, spices, and the like—on the left. The flour bin in the lower left of this view holds more than a hundred pounds. The drawers were for spices and utensils. The cupboard on the right side holds plain white ironstone china, the Kelley's choice for everyday dinnerware. The jugs on the floor below the window hold homemade vinegar, including tomato and sorghum vinegar. The plain white muslin curtains and color scheme, which matches the kitchen, are accurate to the period.

The pantry of the 1900 farmhouse in Urbandale, Iowa, is well stocked with spices, grains, beans, and other dry goods. There are also new appliances, including a potato ricer on the bottom shelf and a mechanical creamer standing in the corner. The two boxes under the bottom shelf held a Conservo, used for canning. Also on the floor are an earthernware jar for pickles and a dasher for making butter.

The most humane contribution that the nineteenth century made to the kitchen, and the most unsung, was window screening. Compared with its contribution to comfort, to sanitation, to the preservation of sanity and good temper, the gas range, the electric range, the refrigerator, and the freezer pale into nothing. Flies were a far worse trial to the housewife of the last century than the pump in the kitchen sink or the scuttle that needed filling with coal. The literature of the nineteenth century household is filled with them.

Russell Lynes:
The Domesticated Americans

Step inside this pantry, and you enter into part of the life and times of a Victorian-era family living in Brunswick, Maine. This is one of the seventeen rooms that were left near to their original state when the last family member shut the doors in 1925. It was kept locked until 1982, when it was re-opened by the Pejepscot Historical Society. The inventory of utensils is so untouched that a glass was found in the kitchen containing a monarch butterfly and a robin's egg.

A journey through the rest of the Skofield–Whittier House envelops one in the world of a prosperous and loving family. Its high Victorian drawing room is hung with crystal chandeliers and heavy velvet drapes, furnished in wicker and brocade, filled with photos, books, and the clutter of three generations. Not only are the furnishings perfectly preserved, so are the accessories, right down to the original toothpaste and soap in the bathroom.

151

Adobe buildings were introduced to the Southwest by Spanish settlers as they moved up from Central America. "Adobe" is the popular Spanish word for mud brick, deriving from the Arabic *el-tob*, dating from the time of the Moorish occupation of Spain. The Native Americans were largely unfamiliar with this 6,000-year-old method of construction, although they had used mud to fill gaps in stone walls.

In traditional adobe building, mud was mixed with a little fine straw and packed into a brick-sized wooden frame, then turned out and left to dry in the sun. Homes were raised on a spot often chosen for the quality of the earth itself. This resulted in a pleasing appearance, with a new home immediately blending into the landscape. The soft curves and smooth finishes on the external and internal walls were often fashioned by the palms of a female hand. Today in the Southwest, there are skilled women artisans called *enjaradoras* eagerly sought to restore the appearance and protective plastering on adobe walls.

Patio areas like in the adobe home shown above were constructed with a purpose. Traditional Spanish builders rarely put a window on the north side of the home but created their patios in an *L*- or *U*-shape, facing south to catch the last sunlight on fall days.

Adobe played an integral part in the construction of log buildings. This stone chimney retains its structural integrity because of the mud used as mortar or plaster to keep the stones in place.

Adding a band of colored earth was a popular method of adorning adobe walls. Colored earths ranged from white, gesso-like washes to soft pastel pinks, blues, yellows, and greens.

Those seeking a traditional adobe residence expect a flat roof supported by its log vigas and a low silhouette. Although controversy still rages in the city of Santa Fe concerning whether an adobe structure with a pitched roof is a valid example of the "Santa Fe style," many historic adobe buildings in downtown Santa Fe have pitched roofs. In northern New Mexico villages, almost ninety percent of adobe homes have pitched roofs.

And it is not surprising, since most flat roofs on adobe houses have to be reroofed every six to ten years, a costly undertaking. Leaky flat roofs cause major structural damage to load-bearing walls, plasters, and interior spaces. The arrival of sawmills and milled lumber in New Mexico in the 1850s caused the local populace, tired of leaky mud roofs, to take to the pitched roofs enthusiastically, especially in the mountain villages.

Much prejudice still exists against the pitched-roof adobe home. It doesn't conform to the Spanish-Pueblo Revival style that demands a flat roof and dominates the Santa Fe hotel and office block skyline. In California, with its long history of adobe architecture and many magnificent historic adobes, flat roofs are more the exception than the rule.

Creators of the "Santa Fe style" took architectural elements from both the Spanish Colonial period in New Mexico and the nearby Pueblo Indians in the 1900s to define an architectural mode. Many architectural historians today argue that the desire to impose this romantic hybrid destroyed many valid architectural types that once gave Santa Fe a greater variety of domestic building designs.

The Old South

The Ordeman House, in Old Alabama Town of Montgomery, Alabama, was built in 1848. This Italianate town house, a typical Alabama half house with a hall to one side and double parlor to the other, was built by Charles C. Ordeman, a German immigrant who participated in architectural endeavors and entrepreneurial ventures in Montgomery during the 1850s. Behind, through the trees, is a two-story original kitchen and slave quarters building adjacent to a row of period outbuildings that served as a laundry, a necessary, and a storage building. Since 1967, Ordeman House has been operated as a house museum by the Landmark Foundation of Montgomery. The city, named for general Richard Montgomery, a Revolutionary War hero, was founded in 1819. Within a few years it was in steamboat communication with Mobile and stage-coach communication with points east. Located in the heart of the rich Black Belt, it quickly became the center of plantation Alabama, a status recognized when Montgomery was made the state capital in 1846, supplanting Tuscaloosa. Five years later, rail-road communications were established both to the northeast and the southwest.

154

The kitchen of the Ordeman House

A Gatefold of Southern Doorways, Facades, and Stairways

Opposite, right

A view into the hall of the Rutherford-Smith-Barman house on the outskirts of Milledgeville, Georgia. Above the door is a fine sunburst fanlight with a spread-eagle motif.

Gaineswood, Demopolis, Alabama, was built by Nathan Bryan Whitfield between 1843 and 1861. Whitfield, a native of Lenoir County, North Carolina, bought land in Demopolis from George S. Gaines and moved his family into the log house on the property. He envisioned an estate that would represent in every way the zenith of artistic achievement. He set up carpentry and plaster shops and used machines of his own design to create this grand estate of Greek revival architecture, for which he acted as architect, engineer, and builder.

The doorway from the main hall into the library of Stanton Hall, Natchez, Mississippi, is one of the thirteen first-floor doorways magnificently carved from pine by John A. Saunders, in Grecian designs taken from Minard Lafever's guide *Beauties of Modern Architecture*.

The central hall of Stanton Hall. The Greek Revival elements were efficiently planned and boldly executed with extraordinary qualities of geometric simplicity and revealed structure. Among the furnishings are two of the original gaseliers, now electrified, probably made by Cornelius and Baker of Philadelphia.

The hall and stairway of the Gordon-Banks House, built near Milledgeville, Georgia, in 1825. Shortly after the house was sold in 1968, in an
extraordinary feat of imagination and logistics it was moved two hundred
miles in sections to Newnan, Georgia, where it was rebuilt and restored.

Right
The magnificent double stairway at Waverley
Mississippi. (See pages 172–177.)

The 1856–57 Lavinia Dabney house in New Orleans was built for her by the famed James Gallier (see pages 164–167). It was rare for a woman to purchase a house, especially in the Garden District, and unfortunately she lost possession just after it was built.

The elaborate wrought-iron two-story porch at Stanton Hall in Natchez (see pages 166–169).

The entrance hall of Andrew Jackson's Hermitage (see pages 184–187) After a disas-
terous fire the house was rebuilt in the Greek Revival style, filled with new furniture from Philadelphia, and the walls hung with new wallpaper that remains today.

Opposite, left
Looking into the entry of Rosedown, Louisiana. The doorway is embellished with a delicate elliptical fan and sidelights.

Right
In the drawing room at Gaineswood, Demopolis, Alabama, the mirrored recess behind the Corinthian columns is duplicated on the opposite side of the room—via mirrors—to create an infinite, playful series of reflections. The matching Italian marble mantels were purchased in Philadelphia in 1853 by Whitfield's son Bryan while he was attending medical school in that city. This room, which Whitfield himself declared "the most splendid room in Alabama," features a veritable forest of columns and pilasters topped with delicately worked Corinthian capitals. Except for the center table and the base of the statue of Ceres, all the furnishings shown are original to the room. Across America at this time there were craftsmen producing furniture in the rococo revival style, some pieces carefully created by hand and others machine-made and clumsy. The universal chair form was the side chair with the "balloon back" produced in enormous quantities in every part of the land; a popular variant of the shape was found in chairs like these with upholstered backs.

In the parlor of Gaineswood, the elaborate plaster ceiling is identical to that in the dining room. Both the dining room and parlor express the house's theme of playful, festive monumentality with their domed ceilings with Italianate plaster ornamentation. Atop each dome a round lantern—a cupola in miniature—is accentuated by diminutive plaster columns and plaster acanthus-leaf friezes. The abundant plaster ornamentation was inspired by designs from pattern books by the architect Minard Lafever. In spite of the rigid classical nature of the architecture of Gaineswood, the romantic attitudes are so pervasive that the austere neoclassicism of the house should be grouped under the term "romantic classicism." During the Greek Revival, the association of the American political system with the democracy of ancient Greece was inspired by sentiment as much as by reason. The late Greek Revival was, indeed, a romantic movement; adopted by the common man as well as the professional, it became the first style in U.S. history to be consciously understood and embraced as a truly national mode of building.

Most of the furnishings in the dining room are original to the house. The silver epergne on the table was made especially for the dining room. The first permanent residents of Demopolis were French refugees, exiles who arrived here in 1817 as a result of the defeat of Napoleon at Waterloo in 1815. A large number of his exiled followers found their way to Philadelphia, where they proclaimed no other purpose than the peaceful cultivation of vineyards and olive groves; they secured from the U.S. government a hundred thousand acres near the confluence of the Tombigbee and Black Warrior rivers and christened the place Demopolis—Greek for "city of people." Despite their foolhardy experiment with the cultivation of grapes and olives, Demopolis developed by 1830 into a town fairly typical of the Black Belt counties of Alabama, where the economy was based on cotton and slavery. (The Black Belt is the swath of fertile prairie that girds Alabama's midsection and takes its common name not from the slaves who once worked its cotton plantations, but from the rich, black, limestone-and-marl soil. This was the heart of Alabama's agriculture. As such, it contained for many years almost all the towns of importance—all located along a major river artery.) The disappointed French colonists eventually dispersed, but their settlement grew into a burgeoning town when ambitious and enterprising pioneers from Virginia and the Carolinas—men like Nathan Bryan Whitfield—between 1817 and 1850 gave Demopolis its first prosperity.

The gardens of Rosedown, near St. Francisville, in the Feliciana country of Louisiana. Rosedown was built by Daniel Trumbull in 1834 and 1835. Along the faded paths and bypaths of the gardens are all sorts of pleasant surprises—niches, footbridges, trellises, and arbors—and formal statues representing the seasons and the continents. Besides the live oaks and pecans that form the planting, there are junipers, azaleas, japonicas, bays, lavenders, and all sorts of tropical plants. Beyond the flower gardens and orchards is a playhouse and schoolroom where the Trumbull children were once tutored by John James Audubon; it is no wonder, therefore, that the library of Rosedown contains an elephant folio edition of *The Birds of America*. It was there that Audubon composed a lyrical tribute to the Feliciana country of Louisiana: "It is where Nature seems to have paused, as she passed over the Earth, and opening her stores, to have strewed with unsparing hand the diversified seeds from which have sprung all the beautiful and splendid forms which I should in vain attempt to des'scribe."

Right

In the dining room an enormous punkah (of Hindi origin: "pahnka," "a large swinging overhead fan suspended from the ceiling or rafters, and worked by a cord") hangs over the table. When operated by a slave this fanlike device provided constant air movement; the airflow both cooled the diners and prevented flies form landing on the food.

Here are two views of the principal bedroom at Rosedown with
its monumental Gothic revival bed. According to family tradition,
this suite of furniture, made by the firm of Crawford Riddell, a
Philadelphia cabinetmaker, had been intended for the White
House if Henry Clay had been elected president in 1844. The
Gothic revival style in furniture was marked by the soaring
verticality and upward thrust of clustered shafts or columns, as well
as pointed arches with pendants below and quatrefoil tracery.

Preceeding page: The exterior of the Gallier House

The double parlor in the Gallier House, in the French Quarter of New Orleans was designed and built between 1857 and 1859, by James Gallier Jr., for his family. As with many New Orleans houses, Gallier House is festooned across its front with wrought iron grillwork, enclosing the upper level of the gallery. In some ways Gallier House typifies the New Orleans town house layout: a side hall runs along one wall, giving access to rooms on the right. In common Louisiana fashion (and in deference to the heat).many of the rooms open onto galleries at the front or rear of the house. On the ground floor of Gallier House, this spacious double parlor is divided by a screen of decorative pilasters and square columns and has an ornate plaster entablature that intersperses stylized foliage and lions' heads. It seems likely that James Gallier Jr. patronized the most fashionable cabinetmakers and galleries in New Orleans. An 1868 inventory lists, in the principal bedroom, a mahogany bedstead, an armoire, a dressing table, and a marble-topped washstand, while in the parlor there were twenty oil paintings as well as marble alabaster statues, including an 1851 bust of the architect's father James Gallier Sr. It must have been gratifying to the young Gallier, given his father's humble beginnings, to don his dinner clothes with gold and sapphire cuff links and entertain the haut monde of New Orleans in his splendid new house. The Civil War brought an end to the boom economy and there was little building in New Orleans during the city's occupation by Federal troops. James Gallier Jr. died in his house on Royal Street on May 16, 1868.

The principal bedroom in the Gallier House, New Orleans. In 1850 James Gallier Sr. relinquished his architectural practice to his son, and the Gallier firm continued to prosper under the direction of James Gallier Jr., and his partner, John Turpin, who had been the elder Gallier's bookkeeper. During the balmy 1850s, the firm designed and built stores, warehouses, banks, a railroad station, and an opera house, as well as numerous residences. During the 1850s and 1860s, the younger Gallier designed a number of notable buildings in the picturesque Italianate style. Since iron was stronger and lighter than masonry, cast iron was widely used by Gallier for the arched windows with hood moldings, decorative brackets, and the graceful Renaissance details for these buildings.

In 1853 James Gallier Jr. married Josephine Aglae Villavaso, whom he met when he went to Saint Bernard Parish, southeast of New Orleans, to buy cypress from the Vallavoso plantation. The Galliers had four daughters and in 1857 he began to build a capacious house for his family. The house is constructed of brick sheathed with stucco, and the first floor is rusticated and painted to resemble granite. It is supported by slender cast-iron columns and framed with lacy ironwork. On the second floor are four bedrooms and a small library. The suite of furniture in the principle bedroom was made by Prudent Mallard, New Orleans's master cabinetmaker, about 1860, and is probably similar to the bedroom suite purchased by James Gallier Jr.

167

Stanton Hall in Natchez, Misssissippi, was built for Frederick Stanton under the direction of Captain Thomas Rose, from 1850 to 1858. With its bold Greek Revival portico of tall Corinthian columns, elaborate cast-iron grillwork, and sumptuous interior, Stanton Hall impressed inhabitants of Natchez from the day it was completed. "The grand front to the south presents a pure Corinthian façade, and might well be taken for a purely Grecian temple," wrote the *Mississippi Free Trader* of Stanton Hall on April 5, 1858; "All the work on the edifice was done by Natchez architects, builders, artists and finishers." The house is constructed of Natchez clay bricks burned on the premises, stuccoed, and pained white.

Stanton immigrated to the United States from Belfast, Ireland, at the age of twenty-one in 1815 and died in Natchez in 1859 a multimillionaire. He made and lost several great fortunes in land, slaves, and cotton, but by 1849 he was extremely wealthy as a senior partner of a cotton commission house. At this time, too, he owned a large number of Mississippi and Louisiana cotton plantations with hundreds of slaves and thousands of acres of land. With this fortune he decided to build a grand new house in Natchez in the latest fashion. The house has impact in both its décor and its spaciousness. A sixteen-foot-wide hallway runs the length of the house—seventy-two feet. Stanton occupied the huge new mansion, first called "Belfast," for just a few weeks before he died on January 4, 1859.

The Natchez region's principal economic resource was the fertile farmland along the Mississippi, which proved to be ideal for growing a new variety of cotton, called "Petit Gulf," first imported from Mexico in 1806. Its yield was very high because it did not tend to rot in the humid, coastal-plain climate as had earlier varieties. This new type of cotton became the white gold of Natchez and the Deep South. After the invention of the cotton gin in 1793, cotton culture spread southwestward. By 1830 the southern states were producing 731,000 bales of cotton; by 1855 the number had grown to 2.9 million; and by 1859 it had reached 4.8 million. Natchez became a center of wealth and culture in the antebellum period, and many of the cotton barons who had extensive landholdings in the surrounding area or across the river in Louisiana built splendid Greek Revival mansions for themselves in the city.

The immense front parlor of Stanton Hall is sixteen feet high, twenty-three feet wide, and fifty feet long. The ornate bronze-finished gaseliers and a pair of morning-glory sconces near the bay, now electrified, were probably made by Cornelius and Baker of Philadelphia and are original to the house. The parlor furniture includes a set of rococo revival chairs and sofas of carved laminated rosewood, possibly made in New York City around 1850, and a mahogany center table in the manner of John Henry Belter. The étagère is of mahogany veneer on New England pine and yellow poplar was also probably made in New York City. The enormous mirrors in the front and back parlors were imported from France. During the eighteenth century, when the Natchez area passed from French to English to Spanish rule, generous land grants attracted settlers, who came down the Mississippi. In 1798, Natchez was named capital of the Mississippi Territory. Further settlement was encouraged when an 1801 treaty with the Native Americans opened the Natchez Trace, a 500-mile wilderness path between Natchez and Nashville. The steamboat era (the first steamboat to serve Natchez docked in 1811) marked the beginning of the city's golden age, at least for those who had enormous cotton and indigo plantations and the slaves to run them. With their slave labor, planters and merchants built an opulent world for themselves, the grandeur of which is evident today.

The mantel in the front parlor of Stanton Hall is one of five magnificent Carrara marble mantels on the first floor carved in New York City and placed in the house by the Natchez firm of Robert Rawes and Henry Polkinghorne. The fireplace still has its original fittings and marble hearth. On the mantel is a pair of mid-nineteenth-century bronze candelabra.

Waverley, on the west bank of the Tombigbee River near Columbus, Mississippi, was built by George Hampton Young in 1858. Among the many southern mansions designed by amateurs, Waverley stands out for its cleverness, its ingeniously simple practicality, and its capacity to take you completely by surprise. Deceptively straightforward on the exterior, Waverley appears to be a two-story house topped by a large, octagonal cupola. Instead of the usual projecting portico, it features an indented veranda supported by two fluted Ionic columns. Young, a cotton planter and land speculator, had migrated to Mississippi from Georgia in 1835. He built Waverley to house his family of twelve, and became a large landowner with some five hundred slaves. After Young's death in 1880, the house passed to his son William. Surrounding the house were not only gardens and orchards but the outbuildings that were the scene of plantation work and Young's enterprises: a brick kiln and lumber mill, a cotton gin, and livestock pens. Though Mrs. Young died before the house was completed, she left it a green legacy in the massive English boxwoods. After the last Young descendant died in 1913, the house stood empty into the 1960s but survived the hiatus in good condition.

Opposite, right

The octagonal entrance hall of Waverley could not have made a better ballroom had it been designed as one, and it perhaps gives a clue to the expansiveness of the man of the house: Southerners who lived in places such as Waverley were great entertainers and fancied themselves not just hosts, but social and intellectual arbiters. One of Young's contemporaries, a fellow planter, wrote that "Young was a man of wealth and high social standing and his elegant home . . . was a center of refined and extended hospitality." Young's modern showplace boasted a built-in china cabinet and secretary, and interior details complemented the spectacular scale of the house. Waverley's rooms displayed all that was fashionable in decoration—sculptural cornices and medallions, marble mantels, woodwork painted with trompe l'oeil effects. Among the original appointments are gold pier mirrors, brass chandeliers, Venetian door glass, an English carpet, and some original curtains.

The entrance hall, looking towards the front door.

The parlor of Waverley. Young, after practicing law, devoted himself to cotton planting with great success—eventually he owned about fifty thousand acres, and his plantations included orchards, sawmills, gristmills, warehouses, and a store. The decoration of his house varies in taste from French to Egyptian revival styles.

The interior hall of Waverley rises four stories to a height of sixty-five feet through a set of balconies and curving stairways, drawing your eye up. The spectacular open hall provides excellent ventilation in the summer by drawing warm air upward in an inspired and successful effort at climate control. Though the floor plan is almost a square, an octagonal core rises from the first floor, so that most interior spaces are made to seem eight-sided. When Young built Waverley, octagonal houses were a fad; in 1848 Orson Fowler published *A Home for All*, in which he extolled the superiority of the octagonal form over the rectangular. The octagon, Fowler said, is close to the sphere, which is the more perfect shape devised by nature herself. Fowler's messianic prose brought forth a wave of octagonal houses in the North, but only rare examples in the South. Here, Young and his architect placed the octagon within the house, creating soaring visual effects worthy of a church. The rotunda and balconies created an impressive stage set for the balls and dinner parties of plantation life in the Old South.

Above is a bed, marble-top dresser, and armoire in a bedroom at Waverley. This set of rosewood furniture produced en suite was made about 1850 by Elijah Galusha of Troy, New York, who had once worked for John Henry Belter. The curvilinear forms and rococo designs of Louis XV's reign were revived in France in the 1830s during Louis Philippe's rule, serving as a nostalgic royal rebuttal to the Empire furniture of Napoleon's regime. This borrowing of past styles and motifs and the mingling of these time-honored ingredients in the eclectic designs of the day was the epitome of artistic conservatism. One critic was moved to remark in *Art Decoration Applied to Furniture*, published in 1878: "The nineteenth century is, without doubt, a great one in many ways . . . and it is not a little singular that in the more personal service of architecture that the kindred art of furniture it should do nothing but revive that which has been done before." This historical revival of the romantic past, begun in the 1840s, reached its zenith during the years immediately following the Civil War.

The Renaissance revival bed in the master bedroom at Waverley was made by Prudent Mallard, the New Orleans furniture maker whose monumental pieces can be found in the splendor of many antebellum mansions of the South. On these pieces a rich vocabulary of Renaissance ornament was carved and applied, wrought in exotic and native woods, by Mallard. This handsomely made half-tester bed has an architectural borken-scroll pediment surmounted by an ornamental crest. In the years before the Civil War, the observant New York diarist George Templeton Strong complained of the "tyranny of custom" that led those who had enough money to spend it on furnishings in the latest French taste. One editor tried to explain to his readers that, in addition to France, Germany, and Spain (not to mention Italy) provided sources of design for the revival of Renaissance styles. However, in the decades that followed the Civil War, the most sophisticated American cabinetmakers, such as Mallard, continued to look to France for models. In their best work they matched the quality of the achievements of Parisian craftsmen.

Preceding page

Rattle and Snap, near Columbia, Maury County, Tennessee, was built in 1845 for George W. Polk, a relative in the famous clan that gave the United States its eleventh president, James Polk. The colorful name "Rattle and Snap" was applied to the estate after it reputedly changed hands several times in one night in the mid 1800s during a gambling game. Rattle and Snap is a pristine example of the architecture of southern nationalism derived from the romantic Grecian of Minard Lafever's *Modern Builder's Guide* (1833). It is a monument to the agricultural boom of the 1840s and 1850s involving corn, wheat, cattle, and the breeding of horses as well as cotton and tobacco. For a century and a half, imposing southern homes such as Rattle and Snap have stood as symbols of the agrarian culture of the Upper South. The stately Greek revival style was popularized in Latin America by such architects as Benjamin Henry Latrobe. It reached a high point of white-pillared grandeur in Middle Tennessee shortly after William Strickland, a pupil of Latrobe, moved from Philadelphia to Tennessee in 1845 to build the state capital. Although the ten colossal columns of Rattle and Snap are Corinthian, an Italianate theme dominates the composition. This theme is evident in the shallow pitch of the pediment and hipped roof, overly vertical proportions, and arcuated windows flanking the entrance.

The double parlor of Rattle and Snap is filled with furniture made by John Henry Butler in the rococo revival style. The most popular of all revival styles in the middle of the nineteenth century, it probably had more intrinsic quality than any of the others. For while it was a new interpretation of eighteenth-century rococo of the court of Louis XV, the nineteenth-century version still adhered to the earlier design vocabulary—the cabriole leg, curvilinear surfaces, S and C curves and scrolls, and shell carving. In the 1840s, design books began to appear in England that showed suites of this furniture, and the fashionable Parisian cabinetmakers of that time had already revived the Louis XV chair. Belter, one of many German-born craftsmen working in New York City in the nineteenth century, is renowned for his laminated and carved rococo revival rosewood parlor and bedroom suites. Although the principle of lamination was not a new one, Belter's method of steaming layers of wood in "cawls," or molds, so that they could be bent and carved into graceful shapes created a distinctive style popular in the South. The sure touch of a mater carver can be seen in the lacy, laminated carving of the cresting rails with the extravagant use of naturalistic curving ornament of carved flowers, leaves, vines, acorns, and grapes.

The music room at Rattle and Snap, by the eighteenth century, had become a mark of social distinction for members of the seaboard gentry in the South to demonstrate an appreciation of good music and even play an instrument themselves. Jefferson enjoyed the violin and collected a fine music library at Monticello, and William Byrd's library at Westover included examples of English and Italian opera. Though formal music in the United States was strongly European-oriented the country also possessed a flourishing native tradition of sacred and popular music. The early colonists and later immigrants brought folksongs with them and either retained them in fairly pure form or adapted them to American conditions. The most widely distributed American music in the eighteenth and nineteenth centuries was undoubtedly the hymn. Evangelical Protestantism made music an integral part of worship. The religious revival was founded not only on the sermon, but the hymn, which provided a sense of group participation and a common fund of musical knowledge. Almost equally strong was a secular, popular ballad tradition, drawn from both native and English sources, and based on the hymn tune.

Opposite
Here the looseness of form of the late 1840s has moved to the tightness and shapeliness of the 1860s and 1870s, from elaborate vine, floral, and fruit motifs to more massive, ponderous proportions and overworked detail. By this time, virtually every historic period was called upon for inspiration, and many different design sources would be incorporated into a single piece. Novelty was the keynote, and designers vied with one another to produce elaborate and showy pieces. The pediment of the bed, with its arched cresting and curved cartouche, has its source in sixteenth-century Renaissance furniture. The meridienne in front of the window was an innovation of the nineteenth century. The Renaissance revival style was characterized by architectural forms, incorporating motifs such as rounded or broken arch pediments in combination with cartouches, acorn trimmings, and tapering baluster legs carved with the exuberance of the preferred woods.

The Hermitage in Middle Tennessee was the home of President Andrew Jackson from 1804 until his death in 1845. A lawyer, soldier, farmer, and politician, Jackson served as the nation's seventh president. His impressive home belies the popular image of Jackson as a rough-hewn man of the frontier. He built an elegant house, one that had an important effect on American architecture: its Greek revival façade won many admirers, inspiring the spread of the columnar style through the Upper South and the West. The farm was aptly named, providing as it did, a refuge from the frequent attacks, both political and personal, that Jackson suffered during the election campaigns of 1824 and 1828. The house seen today is the third Hermitage. Jackson and his wife, Rachel, were living in a plastered, clapboard-covered log cabin when they began building the first Hermitage. A young visitor, Jefferson Davis, described the Jackson's early home as "a roomy log house. In front was a grove of fine forest trees, and behind it were his cotton and grain fields." In 1819 Jackson began construction of a two-story Federal-style house on a site selected by his wife. In 1834 a chimney fire all but gutted the house. When the house was rebuilt, imposing two-story porticoes (front and back) were added with six Corinthian columns and a double gallery.

The front and back parlors at the Hermitage were the center of entertainment. After dinner, Jackson and his guests would adjourn to these two rooms, the men remaining in the front parlor to discuss politics, crops, and business, with the ladies gathering in the back parlor to sew and read aloud. Alfred, who lived all his life on the Hermitage plantation, recalled of Jackson and his daughter-in-law: "Many's the time I've seen General Jackson take Miss Sarah and dance up and down these floors when the parlor was full of company." The furnishings are all Jackson family pieces, most of them dating from the period of Jackson's retirement from the presidency, 1837 to 1845. Many of the items have important historical associations, such as the center table in the back parlor

(seen in the distance), which was presented to Jackson by the citizens of New Orleans in gratitude for saving their city from the British in 1815. The unusual wood-frame leather chair in the library was a gift from Chief Justice Roger B. Taney. A swivel chair, upholstered with horsehair, also in the library, was made of wood from the frigate *Constitution* (*Old Ironsides*) and was originally owned by Jackson's secretary of the navy, Levi Woodbury. The Jacksons had no children of their own, but in 1809 they adopted one of the newborn twins of Mrs. Jackson's brother Severn Donelson and named him Andrew Jackson Jr. When Jackson died in 1845 he left the entire Hermitage estate of twelve acres to his adopted son.

Above is little Rachel's room at the Hermitage. On November 1, 1832, Sarah and Andrew Jackson Jr.'s first child was born at the Hermitage and was named Rachel at the request of her grandfather. On January 25, 1853, Rachel married Dr. John M. Lawrence in what was described at the time as "one of the grandest affairs ever witnessed in this part of the country."

The wallpaper in this room, used by Little Rachel as a girl, is original, and the quilt on the bed was made by her with pieces of silk and velvet in an "exchange" with friends. In the portrait, Rachel, at eighty years of age, is shown wearing the miniature of her grandmother and namesake. Rachel Jackson Lawrence had nine children and lived to be ninety years old, dying in 1923.

The Green-Meldrim House, Savannah, Georgia, was built by Charles Green, a wealthy cotton merchant, in 1856, and was designed by John S. Norris of New York. It was largely constructed of imported materials at a cost of $93,000, which probably made it the most expensive house in Georgia at the time. Architecturally, the Green-Meldrim House is important for two reasons: It is a rare surviving example of an elaborate mid-century Gothic revival mansion in an urban setting, and its extensive verandas and entrance portico are of cast iron. The house is a conventional rectangular block, and all exterior details are Gothic. The deep bay window above the portico is crenellated and has tall, slim perpendicular lights with finely scaled tracery; the other windows and the entrance façade, which are symmetrically disposed, are square headed with Gothic hood moldings.

At the end of summer, 1864, General W. T. Sherman began his famous march across Georgia to the sea, leaving a wake of destruction thirty miles wide and three hundred miles long. On December 21, 1864, Federal troops marched unopposed into Savannah. General Sherman dispatched his famous telegram to President Lincoln: "I beg to present to you, as a Christmas gift, the city of Savannah, with one hundred and fifty guns and plenty of ammunition, also about twenty-five thousand bales of cotton." Charles Green, hoping to save his cotton from confiscation, offered his mansion to Sherman for a military headquarters and played the cordial host. The invitation was accepted, but the cotton was taken, too.

Opposite

The ornamental lavishness of the stucco decoration of the interior of the house seems to have little to do with the restraint of the exterior. The flamboyant detailing in the drawing room is quasi-Gothic in form but incorporates an eclectic mix of baroque and rococo elements. In an era before the profession of interior design as we know it, there were several different options a client could pursue when setting out to decorate a house. Pattern books were the main source of advice; another important resource was the newly created department store. For those wealthy enough to build a Gothic villa on the scale of the Green-Meldrim House, the most common approach was to hire a series of contractors, often under the supervision of an upholsterer, to complete the interiors. The strong individuality of the Green-Meldrim House is typical of all domestic architecture of the Gothic revival. The Gothic designs varied, sometimes dramatically, from region to region, and there were differences even within particular regions, depending on the individual patron, designer, and builder.

Vizcaya, Miami, Florida, was designed for the Chicago industrialist James Deering by the architect F. Burrall Hoffman Jr., with interiors by Paul Calfin and gardens by Diego Suarez, built between 1914 and 1916. More than 1,000 workers were on the payroll at the peak of construction of this seventy-room Italian Renaissance–style villa and its gardens. When completed the house and its grounds required a staff of eighty. Vizcaya served as a winter retreat for the sickly, cultured Deering, a major stockholder in the International Harvester Company. The architect Hoffman, who had worked with Carrere and Hastings, produced an ingenious design for the house with four different elevations, each grand enough to be considered the principle façade. The mansion is meant to evoke a sixteenth-century Italian estate, and achieves its goal admirably. Vizcaya is almost Hadrianic in scale; it cost about as much to build as the Woolworth Building, erected in New York City around the same time. Deering's artistic supervisor, Calfin, designed the interior in the eclectic mode so often seen in great American houses of this period. On travels with Deering, he assembled a magnificent collection of European furniture, artworks, and antique architectural elements. With these he adorned Vizcaya in a four-century progression of styles, from the early Renaissance to the neoclassical.

Opposite

In the east loggia of Vizcaya, the late-eighteenth-century cedar door (one of four), with sculptured bronze decorations and a marble surround, came from the palace in Rome of Prince Torlonia, banker to Napolean. The Torlonia arms are carved at the top of the surround and surmounted by a seventeenth-century Roman bust of Cardinal Albani. Vizcaya's main floor was devoted to large public rooms and entertaining, while the second and third floors were given over to private quarters for Deering and nine elaborate guest rooms and suites, each with a fanciful name such as Pantaloon, Belgioioso, Cathay, or Goyesca. Deering would greet guests in a festive, rococo reception room; then visitors would sit down to conversation in the brooding, shadowy Renaissance hall, dominated by a massive French chimneypiece from the 1500s. Here the beamed ceiling looming overhead is framed by four antique sections of a heavy, carved wooden cornice of the late sixteenth century. The villa Vizcaya, built at a cost of fifteen million dollars, is the grandest mansion in Florida and an outstanding example of the Mediterranean Revival style. A ten-acre, formal Italian Renaissance garden extends from the southern side of the house, studded with statuary, lagoons, and grottoes.

Whitehall, now the Henry Morrison Falgler Museum, Palm Beach,
Florida, was built in 1901 and 1902; the architects were John M.
Carrere and Thomas Hastings, and the interiors were designed by
Auguste Pottier and William P. Stymus. Henry Morrison Flagler, a
founding partner of the Standard Oil Company and pioneer developer
of Florida's east coast, presented Whitehall to his bride, Mary Lily
Kenan of North Carolina, in 1901 on the occasion of their wedding.
Falgler opened luxurious railroad hotels in St. Augustine in 1888 and
was determined to help develop the east coast of Florida as an American
Riviera. In 1895, the many lines making up Flagler's railroad were con-
solidated as the Florida East Coast Railroad Line. That same year his
crews laid tracks to a point just across Lake North from Palm Beach
(later West Palm Beach); the twin ribbons of steel reached Miami in
1896. Finally, after seemingly insurmountable obstacles and more than
twenty million dollars, a 156-mile extension of Flagler's railroad line
reached Key West in 1912, linking it to mainland Florida. The New
York architectural firm of Carrere and Hastings responded to Flagler's
commission with a beaux arts–style house based on the designs made
popular in the 1893 Chicago World's Colombian Exposition.
Whitehall's gleaming white façade, its towering neoclassic columns, and
its tilted, barrel-vaulted roof evoke the days of the Spanish Empire.

Opposite
In the Louis XVI salon of Whitehall. The color scheme of dove gray
woodwork accented by silver was considered rather bold at the turn of
the century. The Savonnerie carpet is in a pattern of entwined flowers.
The mansion's size—fifty-five rooms occupying 60,000 square feet, its
sumptuous interior decoration, and the up-to-date convenience of electricity and central heating—all inspired a New York newspaper to
declare this Palm Beach mansion "the Taj Mahal of North America."
The seventy-one-year-old Flagler spent $2,500,000 to build and
$1,500,000 to furnish Whitehall in the opulent tastes of his third wife,
and yet the house was completed in the amazingly brief period of
eighteen months. The foyer alone contains seven kinds of rare marble.
The guest bedrooms were decorated to represent epochs in world
history, and Flagler's own boudoir mimicked Versailles. The ladies
withdrew to the Louis XVI salon after dinner, leaving the men at the
table with brandy and cigars.

The Beginnings of Suburbia

James Howard Kunstler

IN 1842, THE ARCHITECTS Andrew Jackson Downing and Alexander Jackson Davis produced a popular book of house plans, *Cottage Residences*. The plans formed a schematic basis for American suburban life, and for the orgy of house styles that followed, which came to be bundled under the rubric "Victorian." They also introduced innovations in plumbing and toilet amenities that were practically nonexistent at the time. Downing himself came to argue strenuously in favor of masonry over wood construction, which he said was foolishly impermanent—but his voice was stilled when he died in a steamboat explosion on the Hudson in 1852.

At about the same time Downing and Davis laid the foundation for suburbia, the balloon frame method of construction revolutionized housebuilding in America. Lumber milled to standard dimensions and factory-made nails now made it possible for a gang of semi-skilled laborers to knock together what had previously required skilled joinery. Early doubts about the soundness of the balloon frame house were soon allayed. The practice spread outward from Chicago starting in the 1840s, utilizing the seemingly endless white pine forests of near-by Michigan.

The balloon frame had two profound effects on American house design. First, the ease and cheapness of building in milled lumber encouraged the evermore imaginative articulation of the form beyond the standard orthogonal box. Especially after the huge trauma of the Civil War, houses exuberantly sprouted cupolas, turrets, bays, balconies, oriels, and deep porches in fantastic combinations. These devices allowed the occupants to project both their physical bodies and their imaginations into the transitional zones between the outside and the inside, between civilization and nature. (Houses built on large lots tended to be embedded in greenery.) A girl could lie dreamily reading in a window-seat while lightning flashed beyond the glass; on hot summer evenings families could enjoy a breeze on the porch. The nine-teenth-century American house reached out to the world beyond its walls. It also beautifully demarcated space in a clear sequence of rooms from the semi-public porch to the visitors' parlor to the intimate boudoir.

The styles themselves—Italianate, carpenter gothic, French second empire, Queen Anne, shingle, American Rennaisance—were fugitive expressions of fashion, and they all accomplished the same thing. But Downing's warning about the tragedy of wooden architecture would return to haunt these large houses. Built with cheap labor, richly adorned with milled wooden decoration, they would become maintenance nightmares in later decades.

The inevitable reaction to them anticipated the seismic cultural shifts of the twentieth century: the arts and crafts movement, which attempted to reassert the hand-made against the machine-made, and the "capital *M*" Modernists, who wished to emulate machine forms above the supposed clichés of nature. Frank Lloyd Wright was a peculiar amalgam of both, with an added layer of Japanese influence after he saw that country's pavilion at the 1893 Columbian Exposition. Wright was determined to take the historically vertical house and subdue it into the horizontal. In so doing, he anticipated by a decade the zeitgeist of the sprawling automobile suburb (indeed, later in life he would become one its great proponants).

By the mid-1890s, Wright was producing "prairie style" houses in which densely reiterated patterns in windows, tracery, and embossed masonry were used to decorate land-hugging, simplified, horizontal forms. Gone were the delicate, whimsical extrusions of the post–Civil War era, especially the upward-reaching towers and turrets. In their place, Wright brought severe formality, executed in brick, rock, and concrete slabs, with open interior plans instead of discrete sequences of specialized rooms. Wright's severity extended to the furniture, which he often designed so as to be built-in or immovably fastened to the floor.

In California around the same time, architect Irving Gill anticipated Modernism in stripped-down boxlike stucco houses that owed more to the pueblo and Spanish southwestern traditions than to the European ideology that began to arrive on these shores in the 1920s.

On the whole, however, Americans remained allergic to Modernism in their housing choices right through the great boom of the 1920s, preferring instead houses that emulated traditional styles and methods of construction. In fact, the American house reached its apogee of excellence in the first decades of the twentieth century, when the great innovations of electricity and central heating coexisted briefly with tremendously skilled, affordable workmanship and an active cultural memory of architectural history. Only after World War II, with the launching of the car-based drive-in utopia, would the American house generally be debased from type to stereotype.

The Industrial North

The so-called Wedding Cake House, Kennebunk, Maine, belonged to a sea captain who made his eighteenth-century foursquare home fashionable by adding gaudy architectural Gothic lacework. The Gothic Revival in architecture was literary and sentimental in origin; no sight was more enchanting to the Victorians than a broken castle or a ruined abbey. Romantics in the nineteenth century looked back on the Middle Ages as an ideal period when their valued harmonies prevailed; they wished to revive the Middle Ages and the architecture that went with it. Supported both by nationalism and romanticism, the Gothic Revival began to supplant the Greek Revival and to dominate architectural production in the middle third of the nineteenth century. As with the Greek Revival, the ideas of the Gothic Revival passed down into the vernacular. Gothic-style stone mansions with elaborate projections and recessions of forms were translated into "Carpenter Gothic," in which the stone tracery became wooden fretwork (or "gingerbread") and elaborately pierced bargeboards cut with a scroll saw. The exterior of these new Gothic cottages made the most of the effects of sunlight, shade, and foliage. The architectural pattern books contained only a few drawings of brackets—local carpenters and lumber mills worked out their own fanciful gingerbread designs of scrolls and curlicues, which became the universal design language of the nineteenth century.

Dr. Luke A. Port constructed his elegant home, Deepwood, in Salem, Oregon, in the Queen Anne style in 1894, following the design of William C. Knighton, one of Salem's notable architects of the period. Elaborate in texture and irregular in plan, Deepwood has two stories, a full basement, an observatory, a veranda, and a porte cochere modified for use as a sunporch. The foundation is made of native "pioneer" stone, a sandstone quarried at Pioneer, Oregon, on the Yanguina River near the summit of the Coast Range. The exterior is covered with clapboard and shingle siding in contrasting strata. The roofline is a complex variety of porch and dormer pediments, gable and hipped roofs, and a square bell-cast steeple or tower roof atop the observatory. The

dressed-stone chimney, exposed on the south side, is treated as an important feature of the house. Deepwood features a variety of intricate, original interior details: stained and beveled glass windows, eastern golden oak woodwork, and original 1894 electric light fixtures among them.

Salem, Oregon's capital, was founded in 1840 but grew slowly. Nearly half of its population left to mine California's Mother Lode in the late 1840s. Still in its infancy, the territorial legislature voted to move the capital to Corvallis in 1855 but were stopped by the appropriation of money for a capitol building by Congress. Salem's position was firmly established in 1859 when Oregon was admitted to the Union.

Naumkeag, one of the finest works by renowned architect Stanford White, was built in the Victorian shingle style as the Berkshire retreat of the prominent New York attorney Joseph Hodges Choate and his family. Choate acquired the site—a hilltop with a commanding view of the mountains to the west—in 1884 and hired White to design the house on the advice of an acquaintance, Charles McKim, a partner in McKim, Mead & White. For Naumkeag, White conceived an artful melding of two contrasting styles. The roadside façade imparts a sense of aristocratic status. It recalls a Norman French château, with salmon-colored brick walls, an arched entryway, turrets, and dormer windows that seem to emerge organically from the shingle roof like a set of hooded eyes. In contrast to these smoothed and rounded surfaces, White's masterful, shingle-style rear façade—all angles and broken lines—manages to be both restful and energetic. The design successfully captured the personality of the Choate family—worldly and successful, yet artistically inclined and sensitive to their lovely surroundings. Caroline Choate and her daughter Mabel furnished the twenty-six-room house with antiques purchased largely in New York shops. Mrs. Choate christened the house with the Native American name for her husband's birthplace, Salem, Massachusetts. They translated "Naumkeag" to mean "haven of rest." In 1926, Mabel Choate, who inherited the property after the deaths of her parents, embarked on a remarkable thirty-year landscaping project in partnership with the landscape architect Fletcher Steele.

In the dining room of Naumkeag, on the reproduction sideboard is a pair of knife boxes, probably English. Seventeenth-century Delft and seventeenth- and eighteenth-century Chinese plates adorn the yellow hanging. The reproduction corner cupboard is filled with English lusterware and a Staffordshire tea service with black transfer-printed designs. Joseph Choate's brother and wife gave the service to the Choates as a fifteenth wedding anniversary present. Choate left the interior décor to his wife, Caroline Sterling Choate, who had met her future husband while studying art in Manhattan. She and her two teenage daughters spent months combing New York shops for furnishings and decorative objects. Some of the pieces they chose were antiques, and others were copies and reproductions, all representing an eclectic mixture of styles and periods. Mabel Choate, having helped her mother assemble the original furnishings, wanted to preserve the house just as she remembered it as a teenager. On her death in 1958, she left the house, furniture, grounds, and a large endowment to create a public museum and monument to her parents.

Opposite

In Joseph Choate's study at Naumkeag, above the bookshelves on the right-hand wall hangs an 1895 engraving of Choate's cousin Rufus Choate, who recommended Joseph to his first law firm in 1855. Joseph Choate made his mark in law, successfully arguing in 1895 that the graduated income tax was unconstitutional.
In addition to the study, Nuamkeg has a library filled with Choate's books. Throughout the house are pieces of China Trade porcelain and other ceramics collected by the Choates' daughter, Mabel, who also acquired quantities of Oriental rugs that remain. After the house was completed, Choate achieved ever-greater distinction as advisor to several presidents, longtime ambassador to Great Britain, and friend of both Queen Victoria and her successor, King Edward VII. Though he was active in the practice of the law until his death in 1917, in later life he found more time for his beloved Naumkeag.

Three Houses by Henry Hobson Richardson

The first is Stoughton House in Cambridge, Massachusetts, built in 1882 and 1883. The house was constructed for Mary Fisk Stoughton, the widow of Edwin Wallace Stoughton, a prominent New York City patent attorney who had been ambassador to Russia from 1877 to 1879. She was also the mother of John Fiske—a popular lecturer, historian, and Harvard faculty member—by her earlier marriage to Edmund Brewster Green. (John Fiske, who was born Edmund Fisk Green, had his name legally changed in 1855.) After the death of her husband, Mrs. Stoughton moved to Cambridge to be closer to her son; the Stoughton House occupies a flat lot on Brattle Street. Richardson's plan was an *L* shape, the central hall with the stair located at the junction of the base and stem of the *L*.

Around the central hall are clustered the dining room, drawing room, and library. The service wing is at the top of the *L* stem. A porch at the first floor and loggia at the second are cut into the front of the house. Alterations to the house began soon after its completion. John Fiske converted the second story of the service wing to a library. Later owners extended the house to the rear following designs by Shepley, Rutan, and Coolidge. Glazing of the front porch largely eliminated the feeling of spacial penetration. The sloped roof runs longitudinally, a perpendicular roof with a gable at the base of the *L*. The house was originally sheathed in cypress shingle painted deep olive green.

Opposite and below

The oval staircase with wide, curving steps, which rises in the Brattle Street tower, follows the inside wall of a curved element introduced at the reentrant angle of the *L* shape. A curved inglenook nestles beneath the staircase facing a fireplace. The swelling gunstock posts that form the profile of the wooden mantels recall primitive Colonial forms. The basic components of Richardson's Stoughton House plan include an entrance through the side of the Norman tower with a diagonal vista into an enormous central hall, which incorporates both a fireplace and a staircase.

The critic Clarence Blackall in March 1889 described of the home as "A very delightful, old-fashioned house in Cambridge on Brattle Street, near the Longfellow House . . . delightful chiefly for the rich coloring of the weather-beaten shingles and for the picturesque mass. There is hardly a detail, properly so called, about the whole design: nothing but simple masses, a deeply recessed porch, and a rounded tower in one corner; a dear comfortable looking homestead even if the windows are filled with plate glass."

The Robert Treat Paine House, in Waltham, Massachusetts, was built between 1883 and 1886 and was designed by Henry Hobson Richardson. Richardson's design, which was was actually an addition to the earlier house of 1866, moved several hundred feet west of its original location. But the addition is more than twice the size of the original house, a two-and-one-half-story frame structure with clapboard siding and a mansard roof. Providing a direct contrast with the original, the Richardson addition is lower and much more horizontal in character. Richardson's plan is organized around a central living hall with a huge fireplace and a beautifully carved grand staircase. Around this are clustered Paine's study, a large summer parlor, a smaller autumn parlor, and a dining room. The first story and three round towers are executed in glacial boulders with quarry-faced Kibbee brownstone trim. The second story is sheathed in shingles that flare out to form an offset course above the stone. The main façade, facing a garden by Olmsted, is an open porch beneath a loggia spanning between two round towers. The end façade to the east, seen here, is marked by the large arched opening at the first floor and a Palladian window at the second floor.

Opposite

The uninterrupted interior from the great hall into the tower of the summer parlor enlarges upon Richardson's earlier experiments with the open plan. This plan manifests a major theme of Japanese domestic architecture, as does the subdivision of space in the summer parlor with open wooden Japanese screens. Despite the massive boulders and the seemingly cavelike openings of the exterior, the summer parlor is flooded with light through broad openings that unite the interior with the terrace beyond. The spectacular fireplace with swelling gunstock posts of Sienese marble is illuminated through the screens and spindle work of an inglenook, which, with the rounded bay of the tower, articulates the flowing space. The marble for the fireplaces in the major public rooms was purchased by the Paines in Siena in the summer of 1885, then configured into mantels after Richardson's designs. Stonehurst, as the Paines called their house, stands today as an unaltered record of Richardson's genius.

Above, one of the several curved inglenooks built into the rounded towers.

Opposite

In the enormous great hall, Japanese and Classical Italian themes are carried forward together. The expansive space of the great hall is structurally achieved through a large central ceiling beam supported by an iron tie-rod (secured by an iron washer and nut of bold and primitive design) running from the beam up to the rafters in the attic.

The interior courtyard of the Glessner House, Chicago, executed in brick with granite lintels and sills, is marked by three round projections of varying function and design. Richardson developed the courtyard concept—using the house walls themselves to screen the private space from the street—as an innovative means of protection from real or imagined riots and disturbances in Chicago in the 1880s. This concept, which has the towers projecting into the courtyard rather than exposed to the street, is the dominant element of the Glessner House design. When Richardson reached his professional maturity in his designs of stone-clad urban residences, he began to simplify form and to eliminate archeological detail. He turned instead to basic shapes, continuous surfaces, and the innate qualities of brick, stone, and shingles to create the distinctive architectural quality of his buildings. By 1882, Richardson was recognized as the leading architect in America; even in Europe he had few rivals.

Bottom left

The Glessners furnished the main hall, parlor, and bedrooms with fabrics, wallpapers, and carpets designed by William Morris. Throughout their lives they collected antiquities and handcrafted objects, which, after nearly fifty years of residence in the house, filled every available space. Frances Glessner corresponded at length with the noted Boston collector Isabella Stewart Gardner. Frances and her husband bought important sculpture; Chinese and Japanese bronzes, ceramics, and textiles; as well as Italian and French ceramic and glass objects inspired by antique, medieval, or Renaissance prototypes. They also bought glass objects by Louis Comfort Tiffany and Emile Gallé. Morris and Company furniture adorned the library and schoolroom.

Twenty years after Richardson's death on April 27, 1886, John Glessner recalled him as the most impressive person he had ever met: "He dominated any company where he was, & by his presence only, even if he didn't speak a word. And when he spoke you instinctively felt that he knew the subject he spoke about. . . . He knew his own value & was not afraid to show that he knew it. He impressed every one, even a casual acquaintance as a great big whole-souled, hearty, broadminded, vigorous, forceful man, courteous & affable & with all human & manly qualities."

Opposite, right

Richardson placed the Glessners' library at the junction of the two wings of the *L*-shaped house, as symbolizing the functional center of their lives. Richardson believed in the detailed integration of exterior, interior, and furnishings and was much involved in the interior design of the Glessners' house. Under his influence they came to favor the arts and crafts over the interior aesthetic of their former house. Richardson persuaded them to commission Francis H. Bacon of A. H. Davenport Company of Boston and East Cambridge to create furniture under the supervision of the architect's office. The Glessners' library was designed in the image of Richardson's own library in his house in Brookline, Massachusetts, and the desk was modeled after Richardson's library desk. By 1885 the Glessners owned 2,500 books, most of which were autographed gifts from friends and authors. John Glessner later borrowed the title of one of these books, Viollet-le-Duc's *Story of a House*, for the account of his beloved house he wrote in 1923 for his children.

Writers' Retreats

Entrance hall of the Mark Twain House, in Hartford, Connecticut. Originally neo-Tudor in style, with ornamental details carved by Leon Marcotte of New York and Paris, the front hall was given a completely different character by the Associated Artists of New York (Lockwood de Forest, Candace Thurber Wheeler, and Samuel Colman) in 1881. As the construction work on the house was nearing completion, the Clemenses made the fortunate decision of hiring the brilliant Louis Comfort Tiffany to oversee the finishes of the enlarged entry hall and other downstairs rooms. Son of the founder of the famous New York jewelry firm, Tiffany in 1895 was to found the renowned Tiffany Glass Company (later Tiffany Studios). But in 1881 he was still primarily an interior designer with a special interest in the powerful effect of color. Much of the décor was left to Tiffany's discretion, and the result is one of the most spectacular surviving interiors from the Aesthetic period of American design. The ingenious use of color for which Tiffany is renowned is evident in the base colors chosen for the walls. Stenciled in silver over the handsome rich red in the entry hall were geometric motifs that resembled Native American textile patterns and African symbols as well as decorative elements from India. The house caused much comment in Hartford. As with Clemens himself, it was unusually flamboyant, carrying to an extreme a dominant architectural dictate of the day, "Avoid plain walls at all cost." To William Dean Howells, the house represented Twain's "love of magnificence as if it had been another sealskin coat. . . ."

The library of the Mark Twain House, painted peacock blue by the Associated Artists of New York in 1881. The interior of the house is even more flamboyant than the exterior, the design firm using rich colors and decorative elements drawn from India, the Middle East, Africa, and Asia. Clemens bought the great ceiling-high Scottish mantel in 1874 from Ayton Castle near Edinburgh. It was made for the Mitchell-Innes family, whose crests appear in the overmantel. In the book-lined library, the author read aloud to his family and friends from his own manuscripts, and from Shakespeare and the Brownings; and his children performed

dramas here. A brass plate above the firebox expresses the owner's philosophy. "The ornament of a house is the friends that frequent it." Indeed, a constant round of dinner parties enlivened the house with some of the most important personages of the day—Civil War generals William T. Sherman and Philip Sheridan, journalists Thomas Nast and William Dean Howells, explorer Henry Stanley, and writer Bret Harte. Of this room Clemens wrote in 1892: "How ugly, tasteless, repulsive are all the domestic interiors I have ever seen in Europe compared with the perfect taste of this ground floor, with its delicious dream of harmonious color, and its

all-pervading spirit of peace and serenity and deep contentments." Though he was producing a steady stream of important books in the 1880s—*The Prince and the Pauper, Adventures of Huckleberry Finn*, and *A Connecticut Yankee in King Arthur's Court*—Clemens' lavish entertaining and unwise investments left him unable to maintain the house. To raise funds, he moved his family to Europe and embarked on a worldwide lecture tour.

The William Cullen Bryant Homestead in Cummington, Massachusetts, was built in 1785 and enlarged by Bryant around 1865. Bryant, the first U.S. poet of international stature and for half a century the influential editor of one the United States's oldest newspapers, the *New-York Evening Post*, was born here. In 1872 Bryant's great-grandson Conrad Goddard described the property: "The site of the house is uncommonly beautiful. Before it, to the east, the ground descends first gradually and then rapidly, to the Westfield River flowing in a deep and narrow valley. . . . Beyond it . . . the country rises again gradually, carrying the eye over a region of vast extent." A nearby spring feeds the stream that was the inspiration for Bryant's poem "The Rivulet." The grove of pines, spruce, and hemlocks to the south prompted his "Inscription for the Entrance to a Wood." Bryant knew virtually everyone of importance in his time, both here and abroad, and, although of a reserved, even austere demeanor, he came to be regarded as the first citizen of New York. Nonetheless, he never lost his love for the home of his youth and spent his declining years in the hill country of western Massachusetts.

Opposite

William Cullen Bryant's Study. He never found New York, with its cultivated amateurishness and dillettantism, a wholly congenial environment; the city had something of the atmosphere of Addisonian London and seemed far removed in spirit from the rural simplicity of his beloved Berkshire Hills. In his later years he spent his mornings in this study translating Homer's *Iliad* and *Odyssey*, composing editorials for the *Post*, and writing some of his final verses. Bryant was a traditional American romantic poet who arrived at the shrine of nature through the models of James Thomson, William Cowper, and, particularly, William Wordsworth. As did Washington Irving and James Fenimore Cooper, Bryant celebrated the grand scale and the infinite mysteries of the unexplored western continent. He adapted the Wordsworthian idiom inspired by the vernal wood to his own fondness for the New England landscape, and his rambles in the Berkshire Hills furnished him with material for his verse. But Bryant was more than a nature poet; he was also a poet of his age, who gave strong support to nationalism and had faith in progress.

The Robert Frost Farm in Derry, New Hampshire, a perfect illustration of the connected building pattern of northern New England—"big house, little house, back house, barn." It was home to the young poet from 1900 to 1911. Born in California in 1874 to New Englanders, Frost moved back East with his family when he was ten years old. Frost and his wife, Elinor, had been co-valedictorians at Lawrence (Massachusetts) High School and were already experienced teachers when they moved to Derry. Here Frost taught at Derry's Pinkerton Academy, founded in 1814. His family grew to six by 1905: Lesley, the eldest child, had two sisters, Irma and Marjorie, and one brother. The Frost children were too far from Derry village to go to school, so the horsehair sofa in the front parlor became the classroom. Life and chores on the Derry farm were ordinary enough on the surface, but

Frost's Derry poems deal with his deep love for Elinor, his struggle from despair to hope, and his need to reconcile the cruelties of life with the existence of God. The thirty-acre Derry Farm would be quietly momentous for Frost and for American literature. Long after he had sold the farm to try his fortune in Engand, the poet would write: "The core of all my writing was probably the five free years I had there on the farm down the road from Derry Village. The only thing we had was plenty of time and seclusion. I couldn't have figured in advance, I hadn't that kind of foresight. But it turned out right as a doctor's prescription." In the trunk he packed for England were the Derry poems he would publish successfully there as "A Boy's Will," "North of Boston," and "Stopping by Woods on a Snowy Evening."

This is H. L. Mencken's third-floor office in his brick Italianate row house on Hollins Street in Baltimore, across the street from Union Square. In 1906 Mencken began his long relationship with the Baltimore *Evening Sun*. After hours he set up his base of literary operations in this room. Amid a perennially growing welter of books and papers, he rooted, expostulated, and stormed away on his typewriter. Mencken, then in his prime as a commentator on the literary and political scenes, discharged his artillery at whatever features of American culture struck him as absurd. Through his writing of *The American Language*, his collaboration with George Jean Nathan on *The Smart Set* and the founding of the *American Mercury*, his ups and downs with Theodore Dreiser and his drinking bouts with "Red" (Sinclair) Lewis, and World War I and the crash of 1929, the third-floor room was his kingdom. Though it was barely navigable by strangers uninitiated to the mysteries of its rich, diversified clutter, Mencken insisted that it was "the most orderly room in the house." In the 1920s he introduced into his third-floor office a private secretary to help with his voluminous correspondence, since he was temperamentally incapable of letting any kind of communication go unanswered. Mencken's literary voice as a newspaperman and critic was notoriously impudent and iconoclastic; his maxims and epigrams exploded into the public consciousness like landmines. For instance: "No one in this world, so far as I know, and I have searched the records for years, and employed agents to help me, has ever lost money by underestimating the intelligence of the great masses of the plain people."

215

A Gatefold of Windows and Façades at the Turn of the Last Century

Opposite, right
A side view of the balusters and panelling in the hallway of the Glessner house (1885–87) in Chicago.

The Immigrant Home

Here, and on page 217, are two re-creations of mid 1920s urban Italian-American home interiors, seen at the Smithsonian, in Washington, D.C. These pleasant, old-fashioned rooms illustrate the basic conveniences and comforts in that part of the twentieth century. For some of us, they could be viewed as if we were trying to remember the ambience of our grandparents' home. In fact, this is an accurate repesentation of a modern home in 1925.

The National Museum of American History said of rhe kitchen above " . . . it also stands as an emblem of the way immigrant groups embraced American living standards . . . , for this was the kitchen of an immigrant Italian family, as small details (the clusters of onions and garlic, the oil cruet) show. And yet with all its virtues as a period piece, it bears ample evidence of rapidly encroaching technology. All the signs are there.

Unlike the Colonial kitchens pictured elsewhere in this book,

the room is divided into logical work areas—places to cook, eat, store, and prepare. Instead of an open hearth, there is a gas range (not visible here). On the door is an ice company card, and somewhere in the room there is an icebox with a drip pan—not anything to delight a contemporary kitchen designer but an impressive advance for its day. The Hoosier cabinet against the wall is a rational, if limited, solution to the problem of storing kitchen staples close to the place where they will be measured and mixed. And finally, there is the most modern kitchen appliance of all—the telephone, which both simplifies work and keeps any at all from being done."

The kitchens of the 1920s are a far cry from the futuristic workspaces of the twenty-first century, with continuous hard-surface counters, a battery of color-coordinated under-counter appliances, precisely organized storage cabinets and pantries, the microwave oven, the television, and the home computer.

The three tall entrance doors at Vizcaya, Miami, are
said to have come from the Hotel Beauharnais, the
Paris town house of Napoleon's stepson.

Right
The wide front door of the Gamble House in Pasadena,
California, (see pages 220–225) with its stained glass panels by
Emil Lange depicting a gnarled oak (the Tree of Life).

The Jeremiah Nunan House in Jacksonville,
Oregon. In the 1880s, for about twenty years,
the Queen Anne Style was very popular. It
borrowed influences from all over the world.
It is exemplified by elaborate brick chimneys,
cresting on the roofs, octagonal towers, and
porches and verandahs with straight top arches.

The Green-Meldrim House (see pages 188–189) is a rare surviving example of an elaborate mid-century Gothic revival mansion in an urban setting. Its extensive verandas and entrance portico are of cast iron, and all the exterior details are Gothic. The deep bay window above the portico is crenellated and has tall, slim perpendicular lights with finely scaled tracery; the other windows and the entrance façade, which are symmetrically disposed, are square headed with Gothic hood moldings.

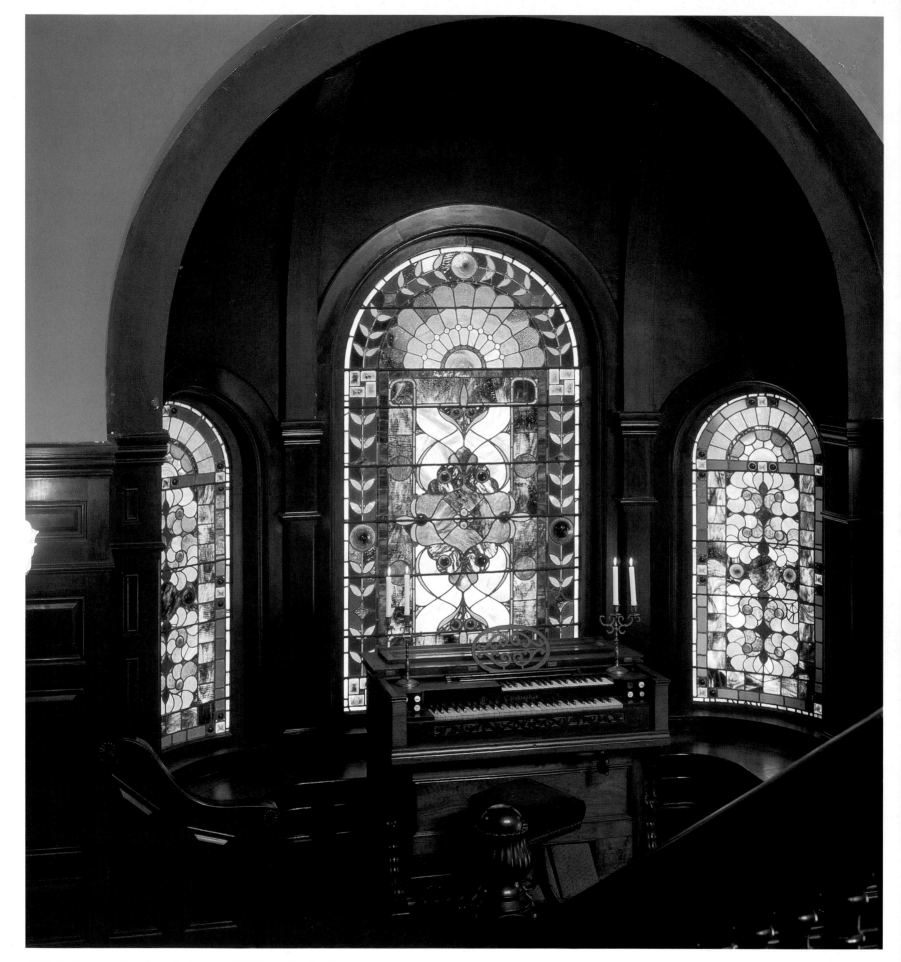

This is the grand stairwell alcove of Wilson Castle, Proctor,
Vermont, paneled in mahogany and with three large stained-
glass cathedral windows. On the landing is a small reed organ.

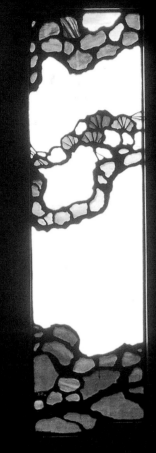
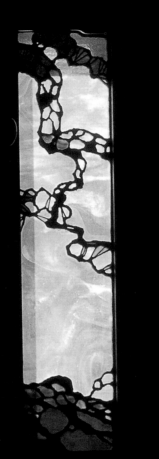

Opposite, left
A view out of the hall and doorway of Rattle and Snap in Maury County, Tennessee, presents a lighter contrast to the rest of the house, which is full of heavy, overworked late-nineteenth-century furnishings.

To own a house was the goal of nearly every immigrant family, indeed of nearly every American. This living room, with its lace curtains, antimacassar on the sofa back, hat rack, and comfortable rocker, could have been home to almost anybody in the mid 1920s. But the newspaper and the keepsakes on the table reflect the Italian origins of the family that lived here.

217

The Twentieth-Century Home

Preceding page, the exterior of the Gamble House.

Wendell Garrett and Michael Webb

Two Views of the Gamble House

The Gamble House in Pasadena, California, designed in 1907 by Charles Sumner Greene and Henry Mather Greene, was built in 1908 for David B. Gamble. The careful interrelationships of the low gable-roof structures of the Gamble House present one of the most sophisticated moments found in the Greenes' extraordinary masterworks. The Gamble site and floor plan went through three fundamental concepts. In the third and final plan, the architects positioned the house parallel to the street, Westmoreland Place, and the garage was placed in the swale of the lower portion of the site along the north property line, discreetly keeping the sounds and activities of the new gasoline-powered vehicles at a distance from the house. To counter the height of the three-level house and the relative compactness of the plan, the Greenes utilized their vast timber vocabulary, creating strong horizontal lines that integrate the building with the site. On the façade, a portion of the second level was cantilevered over the entry. The second-floor roof is low and broad, strengthened by the hovering quality of the smaller third-level roof and by the elongation of the front elevation with the north terrace and sleeping porch. The horizontal railings and broad, low roof are accentuated by the scale and form of the massive structural horizontal beams and outriggers. To the south, the fence and gate structure screening the service yard further emphasizes this horizontality. The transition from building to land is accomplished by a series of terraces and stair landings rather than planting. The long overhang of the roofs keeps the hot California sun off the walls.

The Greene brothers are California's most famous architects of the Craftsman style. They were accomplished craftsmen before they were trained in the profession of architecture at the Massachusetts Institute of Technology. As a result, their buildings and furnishings emanated from a clear understanding of what the craftsman required to realize a design. Additionally, the Greenes were blessed with an extraordinary ability to analyze, visualize, and compose. They were confident, free from tradition, and inspired by the unlimited opportunities for self-expression to be found in southern California. Their engaging and modest manner drew an enlightened clientele with the courage to explore new concepts. Every element within their progressive designs is independent, yet each plays an important role in the total composition.

The entrance hall of the Gamble House is built of dark Burma teak that has been rubbed with oil to create a lasting luster. The three-part front door was designed by Charles Greene and made in the Los Angeles studio of Emil Lange, largely of glass supplied by Tiffany Studios in New York City. In the wake of the popularity of Louis Comfort Tiffany, stained and leaded glass became an important element in the Greenes' architecture. In the beginning the techniques they used were fairly traditional, but they became dissatisfied with the uniformity of stock extruded leading. For variety, they at first cut out patterns on thin sheets of lead and applied them to the stained glass. About the same time—in 1905—they met Peter and John Hall, talented cabinetmakers who would oversee the production of furniture and other interior decorative elements the Greenes designed. It was also the Greenes' good fortune to make the acquaintance of Emil Lange, formerly an artisan in the Tiffany Studios in New York City. Lange came to southern California at the turn of the century and set up his own studio in partnership with another glass craftsman. As with the Halls, a magical kind of rapport quickly evolved between the Greenes and Lange. Charles Greene's demands for more flexibility to achieve the subtleties he desired for his stained glass stimulated Lange. Together they developed a variety of techniques that Lange added to the expertise he had gained from his years with Tiffany.

The furnishings of the living room of the Gamble House, designed by Charles Greene, are made of Honduras mahogany with spines and pegs of ebony. The coffee table in front of the living room fireplace was designed and made in the late 1940s by David Swanson, who had worked on the original living room furniture when he was an apprentice to Peter and John Hall. For a period of time in 1906, the Greenes were strongly influenced by Chinese antique furniture. It was a time of great experimentation and extraordinary attention was given to developing the subtle details of joinery. The decorative, square ebony pegs and pegged ebony spines that became the most identifiable characteristics of the brothers' mature designs emerged first in 1906. The subtle curve of the tops of the pegs standing out above the surface became more sophisticated with each new piece. These refinements resulted in variations among pieces of furniture made for the same client. The quantity of designs turned out between 1903 and 1906 is astonishing, considering that the Greenes maintained absolute control over both on-site construction and the production of furnishings in the shop. It was the Greenes' good fortune to have a number of wealthy clients who allowed them to stretch their talents and imaginations to the fullest. They designed virtually every part of a house, inside and out, as demonstrated by the Gamble House, which represents a totality of control seldom seen in the history of architecture.

WENDELL GARRETT

The entrance hall of the Gamble House.

Almost a century ago, David and Mary Gamble of Cincinnati moved into their new second home in Pasadena. He had retired from Proctor and Gamble, the firm his father had founded, and now joined other wealthy easterners in their annual migration west, wintering at the luxurious Raymond Hotel for four or five months each year. Pasadena had become a fashionable resort, while most of Florida remained a mosquito-infested swamp. Luxuriant vegetation, clear air perfumed with citrus, and the sharp-etched San Gabriel mountains made this an earthly paradise. The Gambles commissioned a woodsy bungalow from Charles and Henry Greene, fellow emigres from Cincinnati, who had been practicing here since 1893. It cost them $50,000—a large sum in those days, but a pittance beside the $11 million that the Vanderbilts spent on their beach house in Newport, Rhode Island.

The Gambles lived here until they died, in the 1920s; ownership then passed to Mary's sister, Julia, and then to the eldest son. The family cherished the house, made few changes, and finally donated it to the University of Southern California, which has lovingly maintained it. A few lucky scholars get to stay here, but all the principal rooms are open for docent-led tours, four days a week.

Other Greene houses in the neighborhood have been stripped or altered; the Gamble is a precious memento of architectural innovation and superb craftsmanship. The late Charles Moore, who lodged here for a few days and then decided to move back to California after years of teaching and practice at Yale, tried to describe its contradictions in *The City Observed*, a Los Angeles guide he co-authored. He called it "mysteriously shadowy and cheerfully candid, special to this place and full of the romance of distant Oriental places, puritanically reticent in its spaces and colors and textures and shamelessly sensual in its wooden members—every one of which has been loved and sanded and softened and rubbed and rubbed. . . ." The Greenes had grown up close to nature, learned to make things at school, and had studied architecture at the precursor to MIT. But the great revelation for them, as for their contemporary, Frank Lloyd Wright, was Japan. All three were impressed by the traditional Japanese pavilion at the 1893 Chicago World's Fair, and sought to incorporate its lessons into their work. Low ceilings, expanses of unadorned wood, a subdued palette, asymmetrical compositions, and the integration of rooms and porches link the Greenes' work to buildings they had seen only in illustrations and felt free to adapt to a radically different culture. They were also part of the Arts and Crafts movement, which the English socialist William Morris had founded to provide an alternative to Victorian excess and the debased products of industry.

MICHAEL WEBB

As architects, the Greenes worked side by side with master craftsmen—including their contractor, Peter Hall, and his brother John, a cabinetmaker. They designed or supervised the making of every structural and decorative element, from staircases to side tables, contoured beams to stained glass windows. Every detail of the Gamble House, outdoors and in, is carefully calculated and adds to the whole.

The Japanese influence is subtly absorbed into the Gamble house, and its open gables, projecting rafters, and stacked balconies seem to have been inspired by a Swiss chalet. The modest facade gives little hint of the riches within. Step through the wide front door, with its stained glass panels depicting a gnarled oak (the tree of life), and you enter an interior that Morris would have adored.

MICHAEL WEBB

Left

The light in the dining room constantly changes because of the rich iridescence of the Tiffany glass in the windows, doors, wall sconces, and chandelier. The dining table and chairs were designed by Charles Greene. The table accepts five leaves without the necessity of separating the pedestal. As work on the house progressed, the shapes remained simple, but straight lines began to soften and the abstract cloud forms found on Chinese furniture began to give a sculptural quality to the Greenes' furniture. Instead of oak and ash they began to use Honduras mahogany, ebony, walnut, and gray maple—woods which could be worked well, took soft stains easily, and responded to the oil finishes the Greenes favored. When designing lighting devices, the Greenes explored indirect as well as direct lighting, wall sconces and lamps, and metal and glass fixtures in addition to the carefully detailed wood and stained-glass fixtures for which they are best known. They also designed hardware, wrought-iron railings, and carefully articulated wrought-iron and plated steel strapping that was integrated with the timber joinery both outside and inside their houses. Logic dictated design, and decoration primarily evolved from the joinery itself. The Greenes drew from the nature of the materials with which they worked, and they understood the tools and crafts of the artisan, so that their works embody the highest aspirations of the Arts and Crafts movement in America. The Gamble House, their acknowledged masterpiece, has been called by one critic "a poem of wood, texture, and light."

Opposite

This is one of several arrangements of living room furniture depicted in pencil sketches of the room by Charles Greene. The library table, with its long, cantilevered writing top, has drawers that pull out from each side. The lamp is from Tiffany Studios. The Greenes' as architects have long been acclaimed, but only in recent years has their talent for designing interiors, furniture, lighting fixtures, carpets, hardware, and stained glass become generally recognized. The interiors are symphonies of rooms and furnishings, materials and joinery, textures and details. No element escaped the brothers' careful scrutiny and the level of craftsmanship is unsurpassed. While Charles Greene is identified as the primary designer of the brothers' furniture, the designs executed by Henry Greene, although fewer in number, demonstrate an equally remarkable sensitivity to scale, proportion, and detail. The Greenes' earliest furniture designs were strongly influenced by Gustav Stickley. The lines are simple and straightforward, and the joinery is emphasized rather than hidden. However, from the outset the Greenes' own touch is evident. Pegs and dowels project from the surface to provide texture and scale, while the beauty and grain of the wood are enhanced by the use of natural finishes. Special attention was given to the hand-rubbed surfaces to prevent discoloration from water marks.

WENDELL GARRETT

The entrance hall, with its stepped brackets and balustrade, pegged paneling and silken textures, is a room anyone would be happy to move into. Beyond, spacious living and dining rooms flow out onto a terrace that overlooks an arroyo. Every surface, every piece of custom-made furniture invites a caress—though the docents will quietly ask you to restrain the urge. Mahogany predominates, but seventeen different woods are employed throughout the house. Every joint is expressed; beams are strapped in steel or wrought iron; cabinets are inlaid with flowers of abalone shell and silver. Lustrous and rich-toned stained glass from the Tiffany studio provides accents of color throughout the dimly lit interior. The plan is quite traditional, for the Gambles had a passion for privacy. There are fifty doors in the house—five in the kitchen alone—but in some ways the house is ahead of its time.

There are openings throughout to allow cool breezes to pass through, and the wide eaves create pools of shadow that make air conditioning unnecessary on all but a few days in summer. The porches were intended for sleeping outdoors on summer nights— Los Angeles was hotter then than it is today. Though the Greenes priced themselves out of the market by insisting on refined hand-craftsmanship, their bungalows set a model for informality and restraint and became part of the southern California vernacular. Builders' copies line the streets of early-twentieth-century neigh-borhoods, and some fine hand-crafted examples survive, but noth-ing rivals the quality of the Greenes' work. A single chair from the Gamble house would now sell at auction for more than the own-ers paid for their entire residence in 1908. It's another example of how great architecture and design bring lasting delight and make the best of investments.

MICHAEL WEBB

Three Early Masterworks by Frank Lloyd Wright

Oak Park Home and Studio in Chicago was built between 1889 and 1898. This was the first of three house-studios that Wright created for himself, and it anticipated Taliesin, Wisconsin, and Taliesin West, Arizona, as a laboratory for his ideas and a showcase for his art. Wright was head draughtsman at the prestigious Chicago firm of Adler and Sullivan when, at the precocious age of twenty-one, he borrowed money from his mentor, Louis Sullivan, and built this house for himself and his future wife, Catherine Tobin. Over the next twenty years they had six children, and Wright added a playroom in back and a studio to one side.

The house takes its place comfortably alongside other Arts and Crafts residences on a wide leafy street in Oak Park. But the architect's signature is already apparent in the shingled gable that dominates the west front, the square cornice that juts from the octagonal library, and the ground-hugging studio. The seed of the Prairie houses germinated here, and the closer you look at the lines and details the clearer it becomes that Wright is asserting his mastery of a familiar style and moving beyond it. The additions yielded a cross axial plan, and the rooms began to acquire a distinctive personality and to flow into each other, fusing family and work life. Aided by talented assistants, Wright designed 125 buildings here—a quarter of his life output, including some of his best—between 1898 and 1909, when he moved out.

Miraculously, the house survived sixty-five years of disruptive alterations, before a foundation was set up to restore it to the way it looked in 1909 and to maintain it as a public resource. It is deeply rewarding to explore how Wright's genius flowered in his first decade of practice. The oak stair that flows down through the foyer as though pushing out of doors is an early example of his gift for dynamic movement, and the barrel-vaulted playroom (which doubled as a gym, kindergarten, and performance space) demonstrates his ability to combine traditional warmth with structural daring. The lighting, art glass windows, furniture, and inspiring inscriptions all contribute grace notes to the whole.

One of the greatest and certainly the most famous of the Prairie houses Wright designed in the first decade of the twentieth-century is the Robie residence in Chicago. This work illustrates Wright's goal of marrying his buildings to the midwestern landscape. This was the land of his childhood—he was born in the Wisconsin countryside and spent many months working on his uncles' farms. As a romantic, he dreamed of fields rolling away to the horizon; as an architect, he sought to bring that spirit to suburbs like Oak Park. To symbolize an open horizon that no longer existed, he used wide sweeping eaves, horizontal bands of casement windows, and striated brick walls that extend outwards from the houses themselves.

The Susan Lawrence Dana House was one of the first and most luxurious of this new breed, a thirty-five-room mansion that defies the constraints of its conventional urban site in Springfield, Illinois. Commissioned by a wealthy heiress who had recently been widowed, it was designed as an intimate residence and a spacious salon in which to entertain society on a lavish scale. The low walls of gray Roman brick, set off by buff cornice lines, serve as a foil for the bronze green plaster frieze in which the angularity of stylized sumac plants anticipates zig-zag moderne reliefs. The façade is also animated by the eaves, which tip up at the corners—a feature that Wright borrowed from the traditional Japanese house he visited at the World's Columbian Exposition of 1893 in Chicago.

Wright took full advantage of his client's generous budget to create an opulent interior in which the richness of the decoration belies the simplicity of the lines. The entrance hall, gallery, and dining room are soaring, multi-story spaces with boldly arched vaults—an astonishing shift from the emphatic horizontality of the façade. Stained glass windows and screens in mellow golds, greens, and oranges evoke the vegetation that is absent on the built-up site, and these colors are picked up in the textured plaster walls and reddish stain of the joinery. You feel as though you are strolling through a forest in fall, the trees hung with sparkling jewels. Wright designed over a hundred pieces of furniture and light fittings for this house, some of which have achieved classic status are now in production. Mrs. Lawrence lived here for twenty-five years; astonishingly, the house remained empty until it was bought by a publishing company in 1944. It has since been meticulously restored and is maintained by the state of Illinois.

234

Aileen Barnsdall was the daughter of a Pennsylvania oil tycoon. She was a rebellious heiress who was intent on producing avant garde drama, first in Chicago, then in Los Angeles, where she bought a thirty-six-acre hill on the edge of downtown. She was introduced to Wright and commissioned him to design her a house just as the architect was becoming more deeply involved in the creation of the Imperial Hotel in Tokyo. In the days before air travel and email, he might as well have been on the moon, and the correspondence with his demanding client stretched out over three years until they were able to agree, in 1919, on an ambitious plan. Little by little the house was built: an augury of Wright's least productive decade. He struggled but failed in the 1920s to revive his flagging career in southern California, despite the explosion of new construction and a sprinkling of maverick clients who were receptive to new ideas.

The Hollyhock House, named for a flower that grew on the site and inspired the stylized finials, is an anomaly in many ways. It sits atop the hill, commanding a 360-degree view, even though Wright made a principle of siting his houses below the brow. It has the quality of a Mayan temple in the contrast between spacious courtyards and modest interiors, the decorative frieze playing off a battered upper story, and the compressed entry loggia that is terminated by massive concrete doors.

Expansive in scale and as exotic as a set for Indiana Jones, the Hollyhock House looks forward to the four small textile-block houses Wright would build in the early 1920s, prototypes of an American architecture with indigenous roots. Yet the Hollyhock house is of hybrid construction—precast concrete alternating with more conventional wood-framed stucco.

Cross axes running north-south and east-west intersect at a loggia looking into a semi-enclosed court and an amphitheater beyond, so that the house has a hollow core. The true center is the living room, with its shallow pitched vault. The hearth was always the symbolic hub of Wright's houses, and here it is the focus for a celebration of the four elements: air in the form of light streaming from above, the stone hearth, and a pool around its base fed by a channel from the water court. The relief on the mantel is intended as a pictogram of Aileen Barnsdall as an Indian princess, sitting on a throne, gazing out over the desert to distant mesas. Built-in benches face the hearth and the room is enhanced by Japanese screens from Wright's own collection.

The master suite, which has lost its original furnishings, is on the second floor, looking out over an expanse of roof terraces. The city of Los Angeles is custodian of the house and is currently undertaking a major restoration to remedy its years of neglect and damage dating back to the 1994 earthquake.

Houses and Housing in the Late Twentieth Century and Beyond

Denise Scott Brown

IN THE EARLY 1920S, the young Le Corbusier designed a small house for his mother and a hypothetical city for three million people. During the 1930s, Frank Lloyd Wright formulated his modest Usonian house and vast Broadacre City. Architects tend to view these bipolar \visions of the two masters as defining moments in twentieth-century housing, and it is true that they became models for housing design and ideas on urbanism for architects worldwide. Although Wright's and Le Corbusier's cities were to be designed by one architect, themselves, few architects today would conceive of a whole housing environment as the work of one person, or even one team. But architects still tend to forget that the great majority of houses in the United States are not designed by architects. The major producers of housing are merchant builders. Some well-known architects do influence builders' designs, and history provides further models—and of course, the housing supply at any one time consists primarily of existing houses of different ages that have been altered over the years by their occupants, to meet their needs and tastes.

Arguably, the principle housing event of the twentieth century was not the introduction of the flat roof, or publication of the *Ville Radieuse*, or even the advent of the "split-level rancher," descendant of Wright's Prairie houses; it was the build-up of housing that accompanied the post–World War II transformation of American cities. World War II was a housing watershed. Thereafter suburbanization became a major trend. Pushed and pulled by factors that included the availability of subsidized home loans, low-cost automobiles, and a fast-growing regional road network, people left cities for the "countryside." Automobiles allowed the filling-in of land between rail lines that radiated from cities. Starting in the 1950s, first housing was built, then related community facilities, and later office parks, regional malls, and many of the appurtenances of urban life. These spread out on a vast scale beyond city boundaries, as a new balance was established between urban and suburban activities, a balance based on the availability of the automobile.

The icon of the mass suburban housing of the 1950s and 1960s was Levittown. This southern New Jersey community of single-family detached houses, one of three built by Levitt and Sons in the 1950s, was located within fifteen minutes' drive of various work opportunities, including a large steel plant. Levittown's curving roads lined with small, pitch-roofed houses came to stand for "urban sprawl," with its supposedly conformist population and monotonous architecture—everything people hated about the mass society. Early Modern architects had thrilled to a vision of mass-produced houses rolling off the conveyor belt the way automobiles did: the house as Model-T. In fact, housing was never industrialized in this way, nor was it built by giant corporations. It remained tied, as it had been historically, to regional rather than national economies and markets. The merchant builders who housed the returning veterans and created the postwar suburb were, with few exceptions, small-scale private-sector operators who rarely built more than one hundred houses a year.

240

"These houses are all alike, they just look different."

Merchant builder's ad, 1960s

Prefabrication of housing, another preoccupation of the early Modern architects, was experimented with in America and elsewhere after the war. It produced hopeful visions but not much reality until the private sector introduced trailers and trailer parks, now an important facet of American housing. Industrialization, though not on the Ford model, was achieved to some extent by the largest homebuilders, who tended to integrate vertically, owning some of their suppliers and warehousing to avoid delivery delays. And industrial production of some components of housing increased, although to the extent these mimicked historic, hand-made elements—for example, clip-on plastic Classical moldings—they were not easily recognizable as industrial.

In Europe, major rehousing after World War II was undertaken by government, through the reconstruction of bombed areas in old cities and the creation of new cities beyond existing city lines. Architects designed the majority of such housing. In the United States, a very small proportion of all housing was built by the public sector. The equivalent of "council housing" in England was produced in America by private builders. Government's role was limited to enabling activities, such as the subsidy of loans to homebuyers and the provision of roads and utilities. What public housing was built in the United States was designed by architects in the manner of European high-rise proletarian housing. But architects whose commitment to social housing led them to employment in the public sector found almost no opportunity to work as designers and implementers; they tended, instead, to become "housers," pushing economic programs and devising financial support mechanisms for low-income housing.

By the end of the post-war building boom, housing had become a regional commodity that the emerging computer technology could map and model as a sector in the economy. The housing equation included variables such as the price of land, the cost of the drive to work, property taxes, and a hard-to-measure value for amenities and neighborhood image. Builders tended to build for markets and market segments. Formally or informally, they profiled their customers, trying to understand their tastes and values. This could result in glowing ads for "new communities" set among parks and recreation facilities, or merely in individual units, superficially varied and styled to represent an image the builder thought would appeal to buyers. Although housing was a market commodity for builders, many showed more discernment for people's requirements than did visionary architects of the postwar period, whose urban images prescribed housing for "the masses" as Ford prescribed the Tin Lizzie: the same factory-made unit for everyone.

Trade journals, householders' do-it-yourself magazines, women's magazines, and architecture monthlies tuned to high-income buyers helped the homebuilder make design choices. This literature gives a fascinating view of the emerging lifestyles of the American middle classes over the span of the twentieth century. Ads for housing, furnishings, appliances, bathrooms, and kitchens throw light on changing needs and tastes within the society. The houses too, as supplied and styled by builders, can be read as social documents. At times styling became a community décor de la vie. For example, in Houston in the 1970s, when the city was one of the fastest growing in the United States, newcomers could buy instant atmosphere and context with their houses. New developments were themed to look like Mediterranean Spain or Georgian London and given names like "Trafalgar West."

241

Historical allusion was not intense in Levittown as originally built. The early community projected a generic, stripped-down Cape Cod image, but occupants hyped the imagery as they altered their homes to meet both functional and symbolic needs. Levittown today (renamed Willingboro) seems far from its conformist image of the 1950s. Landscaping has grown, garages have been converted to living space; all manner of applied decorations attest to the attitudes and values of the individuals who live there. From the furnishings of the living room to the eagles and wagonwheels of the front door and yard, suburban interior and exterior styling is dependent on what is available from the local hardware or home supply store.

Today's suburban housing tissue, like that of the medieval town, occupies the interstices between the large-scale, technology-dependent systems—the transportation systems—that help shape the broader region. The crystal-like structure of most urban tissue, from the Greek polis to the Italian hilltown, from residential South Philadelphia to modern Tokyo (based as it is on ancient subdivisions), derives from the most economical widths for spanning wood roofing over houses. The technology of roofing calibrated the city for more than 2,000 years. Yet, although suburban house roof spans are remarkably similar to the ancient ones, roofing technology no longer shapes the suburban environment. A new adjudication between the technologies of transportation and home-construction allowed housing to be set within the looser, less dense environment permitted and required by the automobile. Single-family detached houses, spaced apart, with yards back, front, and sides, approximated, as well, to the American Dream—to peoples' image of the good life in a rural setting, with home a pitched-roof cottage on a winding road—although this dream was not considered by the literati to apply to the "ticky tacky boxes" of suburbia.

Fifty years later demography, technology, and values have shifted. The three-child nuclear family is no longer the only, or even the major, American family form. An aging population is demanding a reformulation of housing types. An increasingly diverse population is influencing the vision of what constitutes a good home, as earlier immigrants did before them. Work places have joined housing and retail uses in the suburbs; density and mass have developed within the sprawl; and suburban transportation facilities have grown even larger, to provide access between spread out but intense population centers at the edges of cities. This new form of urbanism has been named "Edge City." Although suburbia is no longer seen as the only purview for the good life, evidence suggests that it is still the one preferred by most groups. Places like Willingboro are considered a desirable option in progress upward by today's inner city populations, as by others before them.

Since the last decades of the twentieth century, another new technology has threatened to alter once more the balance between moving and staying put and the relation between work and home. The personal computer has caused the term "cottage industry" to be reinstated and has given rise to discussion (but not yet much action) on its possible role as a determinant of urban form. If the major focus of the Internet were to shift from information highway to shopping mall, this could alter the urban balance yet again.

Changes in the role of women, particularly the influx of married women into the work force, have affected lifestyles at the turn of the century. Daycare out of the home and evening shopping are two results; the humanizing of the workplace is another. In the early twentieth century, the aim of both housewives and Modern architects was to produce a more work-like home; at its end, working women were trying to create a more family-friendly, home-like workplace, where you could take your daughter (and, as we humanized further, your "child") to work with you. Once home, two-bread-winner families of the 1990s seemed intent on creating a comfortable respite from the working world. Bedroom, bathroom, and kitchen retail chain stores proliferated. A spate of baby making, nest building, and home construction accompanied the roaring economy of the late 1990s. The large houses on large sites of dot-com suburbia suggested Levittown on steroids.

A rekindling of interest in historic house preservation in the 1970s brought architects in line with the general population, who have always liked Williamsburg. Architects departed this trend (for a second time) in the 1990s, leaving, I suspect, the general population still with it. Ecology and the Green Movement played themselves out in homebuilders' ads and in people's lives, although green technologies such as solar power have not been easily introduced into housing. The success of the anti-sprawl New Urbanism movement suggests that the general population may now be joining the architects in hating everyone's house in suburbia except their own.

What of the future for houses and housing? At the dawn of the twenty-first century, change in housing is difficult to predict, particularly change in suburban housing. Will women now leaving the corporate workforce and set up their own small businesses at home? In what proportion? How will women and men further organize to maintain family life while both spouses work? Will daycare become a neighborhood concern? Could one solution for inner-city families, particularly single-parent families, lie in the development of small units within large old houses, where some functions, for example daycare, could be handled cooperatively? Will the increased prosperity of some groups lead to the expression of more diverse sets of values in the suburbs? Will single people want to rent in the suburbs? Will the New Urbanists succeed in turning around suburban housing culture to support relatively dense communities contained by green belts? Would these be different from Levittown in their ecological effect on the region, or in the transportation demand they generate, or the facilities they offer residents? What new architectural models will arise in the future? Will present relationships among the technology of movement, the workplace, and the residence—or between political structure and tax structure—hold into the twenty-first century, or will the balance change once again? The only certainty is that all these variables will bear on housing.

A great city should offer its residents a multitude of housing choices, modest and luxurious, to satisfy those whose incomes, lifestyles, cultures, and ages, vary widely. To achieve this, some kind of regional housing strategy, set within a regional economy, would be necessary. In modeling this strategy, choices should be set out according to the myriad groupings through which urban society can be defined. No architect or planner can produce a single vision for arriving at this end, but urban plans can help set goals, suggest options, and devise guidelines. A good strategy should allow for unexpected contingencies and for the unpredictable leaps—of faith, style, and technology—that make a city vital.

243

The essence of architecture can be said to be honesty of expression and purity of form. Rarely in the history of civilization has this essential content been found. Some examples may be ancient Greek, medieval Gothic, early American Colonial vernacular, and Shaker architecture. In our own epoch, Frank Lloyd Wright, Le Corbusier, Mies van der Rohe, and others certainly provided this quality.

The modern movement (from 1920 to 1960), came closest to this expression by combining form and technology in its purest sense. Modern architecture of this period also gave evidence of the optimism and idealism that marked an extremely important phase of global intellectual and cultural development. Its roots continue to nourish.

RICHARD BERGMANN

Idealism and the Modern Movement

Rudolph Schindler moved from his native Vienna to Chicago to work for Frank Lloyd Wright. He relocated to Los Angeles in 1920 to supervise construction of the Hollyhock house, then launched his own practice. The house-studio he built for himself and his bohemian wife, Pauline, is still one of the most daring experiments in living ever constructed. Tilt-up concrete panels separated by narrow glass strips support a flat redwood roof, and sliding glass doors open onto outdoor rooms defined by hedges. As Schindler explained, each person would receive a large private studio, while each couple that visited would share an entrance hall, a bath, and an enclosed patio with an outdoor fireplace. There were open roof porches for sleeping and a shared kitchen. A tall screen of bamboo fences the house off from the traffic on Kings Road and the apartment buildings that now crowd the empty field that Schindler found.

The concept of a cave with a canvas screen across the opening was inspired by a camping trip to Yosemite, and Schindler naively supposed (as did the Greenes, Wright, and other newcomers to the area) that one could live and sleep outdoors year-round in the benign climate of southern California. The idea of outdoor living rooms, warmed by open hearths, was seductive, but winter rains, spring fogs, and chilly nights drove the residents indoors; trying to sleep on the roof brought the same result.

Though the utopian plan provoked endless tensions between the Schindlers (who formally separated, and communicated by pushing notes under each other's door) and a constant stream of artistic tenants, it fulfilled its maker's vision. The house cast a spell, and shaped lives; it is full of passion and promise for Rudolph Schindler's later work. Miraculously saved from redevelopment, it was lovingly restored by the Friends of the Schindler House. The intangible qualities of the house are as important as the structure. Wandering through the empty rooms as the late-afternoon sun streams through the high windows, or attending a candlelit reception in the garden, it is easy to conjure the ghosts of the artists and musicians who performed and argued here over the fifty years that Pauline kept her salon. The house continues to serve as a focus of the avant garde under the direction of the Museum of Decorative Arts in Vienna, which is funded by the Austrian Government and here honors a native son.

No architect did more to popularize modern architecture in America before the second world war than Richard Neutra—a master of the flat-roofed, white stucco box that opened up to nature through expansive windows and sliding doors. Born in Austria, he was a friend of Schindler's in Vienna and followed in his footsteps—first to Chicago, then a few months in Wright's office, and finally, in 1925, to Los Angeles. "In Southern California, I found what I had hoped for," he later wrote, "a people who were more 'mentally footloose' than those elsewhere, who did not mind deviating opinions…where one can do almost anything that comes to mind."

Richard, his wife, Dione, and their first son moved into the Kings Road house and the two men collaborated for a few years before Schindler angrily dissolved the partnership. A principal cause of the rupture was this extraordinary house, finished in 1929, which was built by Neutra for Philip Lovell, an eccentric self-taught doctor who prescribed exercise, a healthy diet, and nude sunbathing in lieu of drugs or traditional remedies. His newspaper column brought him fame and fortune, and he commissioned three houses from Schindler, including a surviving masterpiece in Newport Beach. Experimental designs were good for his image, but he was intolerant of the inevitable flaws and cost overruns. The beach house leaked and the mountain cabin collapsed under the weight of snow.

In 1927, he bypassed Schindler and commissioned Neutra to remodel his offices and then to design his new town house, known as the Lovell Health House, in Los Angeles, on a precipitous hillside. He was delighted with the result, telling his architect: "you have created a masterpiece . . . for nearly two decades a house of comfort, happiness and, above all, radical drugless health." In the reel Hollywood, though, only villains appreciate modern architecture; the Lovell house was recently featured in *LA Confidential* as the home of an arch criminal.

The image that made the house so famous and launched Neutra's career is a stack of white stucco decks that appear to float off a rugged hillside on the western edge of Griffith Park. To achieve this dizzying structure, Neutra drew on his experience of building large hotels for the firm of Holabird and Root in Chicago. He designed a lightweight steel skeleton that was fabricated in sections and trucked to the site, then welded and assembled on reinforced concrete foundations in just forty hours. Ribbons of steel sash windows form part of the structural frame. Open sleeping porches (later enclosed) and balconies are suspended from the roof frame. Concrete was hosed onto steel mesh to form the floors and roof.

The low entrance at the upper level gives no hint of the size or drama of the house. The present owners bought it not for its architectural fame, but because they had a large family and the house has five upstairs bedrooms. An open-sided staircase, lit by Model-T headlights embedded in the wall, leads down into a double-height living room that is bathed in light from the huge expanse of glass to the south. For a house that has been intensively used for over 70 years, an astonishing quantity of the original built-in furnishings remain, and are now carefully preserved. Beneath the entrance is a library, ahead is the dining room and kitchen. More stairs lead down to the pool and on to gardens and an exercise court. The easy flow of space from indoors to outdoors has become a staple of southern California living, but it was Neutra and Schindler, immigrants from a cold country, who first took advantage of the benign climate.

254

The Saarinen Home and Studio, in Bloomfield Hills, Michigan, was built between 1928 and 1930. Great architecture and design is a deep-rooted tradition in Finland, and Eliel Saarinen made an important contribution to his native country before entering, and narrowly losing, the 1922 competition for the Chicago Tribune Tower. His second-place design was acclaimed, and he decided to stay on in the booming American Midwest. George Booth, a prosperous businessman with a fresh vision of how the arts should be taught, invited him to become master planner and director of the Cranbrook Academy of Art, a complex he founded on his estate in a leafy suburb of Detroit. Early on, Saarinen built a row of houses for the principals of the school, including this spacious home for himself, his wife, Loja, and their son, Eero.

In the 1950s, he would create his iconic tulip chairs and tables and build such spectacular modern landmarks as Dulles International Airport and the TWA Terminal at New York's Kennedy Airport, but the older Saarinen had more traditional values. The red brick façade of the house, with its tiled roof and leaded windows, as well as the walled sculpture court in back, recall the domestic architecture of William Morris, the English pioneer of Arts and Crafts, whom Saarinen and Booth both admired.

259

The interior is much more progressive, despite the red velvet curtains that can be drawn across the entrances to the principal rooms. There are few doors on the ground floor, and the open light-filled volumes flow one into another: a spacious foyer, library, living room, and studio. Only the octagonal dining room, with its softly glowing fir paneling, Chinese red niches, and shallow gilded dome, suggests a Scandinavian country house of the early nineteenth century.

To introduce a more contemporary note, Saarinen designed elegant chairs and a round table in inlaid wood that strongly echo the elegant Art Deco designs that were then coming out of Paris.

All three members of the family contributed to a house that has one foot in the past and one in the present—as did the father's monumental train station in Helsinki and his design for the *Tribune*. Loja wove rugs and fabrics, and Eero designed silverware and some tubular metal chairs that would have seemed right at home in the Bauhaus.

Opposite, right
Saarinen's desk occupies one of the raised alcoves at the ends of the long, barrel-vaulted studio, which doubled as a reception area.

Cedric Gibbons, the supervising art director of Metro-Goldwyn-Mayer Studios in its glory years from the 1920s through the 1950s, was the epitome of style. On screen, he would have been played by William Powell: a lean, dapper figure with an impeccably cut suit, gleaming shoes, jaunty homburg, and kidskin gloves. His taste created glamorous settings that often shone as brightly as the studio's stars, and he created the Dolores del Rio House, in Santa Monica, California, in 1931 as a love nest for himself and his new wife, the Mexican star Dolores del Rio. Though the 5,000-square-foot house was partly designed by Douglas Honnold, an architect who worked at M-G-M and later began a residential practice, the concept is pure Gibbons in its mastery of scenic effects. It is an enduring memento of a short-lived infatuation with sleek modernity as the embodiment of sophistication and chic. Recent owners have restored and maintained the house in pristine condition.

SLOBBERIN DRUNK
AT THE PALOMINO

The house is located on a quiet, dead-end street and is surrounded by a walled garden. The street facade is as bare as the wall of a studio sound stage, focusing attention on the gray metal door with its asymmetrical frame of angled setbacks. You pass through into a light-filled reception room, looking out through horizontally framed windows to a palm-shaded terrace, which steps down to a pool. Light gleams off polished black linoleum, stepped white walls and ceilings, and the nickel-plated steel stair balustrade. The staircase has shallow white terrazzo treads, is silhouetted against the far wall, and was made for eye-catching entrances. The star would descend from heaven to greet her guests and to lead them back up to the expansive, second-floor living room with its step-vaulted ceiling. Leather club chairs and flared torcheres punctuate a space that could stand in for a 1930s night club. You half expect Fred Astaire and Ginger Rogers to saunter on, glide across the floor, and whirl away in dizzying turns.

Gibbons delighted his bride with concealed lighting, the illusion of a full moon on a white wall, and a summer shower that pattered on the copper roof whenever a sprinkler system was activated. However, there is much more to enjoy in this house than ingenious effects and luxurious details. In contrast to the shallow deception of a movie set, which becomes habitable only on screen, and the geometric austerity of contemporary European modernism, this is a house that rewards the senses as well as the intellect. Spaces are layered and varied, and wall mirrors add another dimension to each room. The house is rectalinear, except for a curved passage that leads to a breakfast room with a shallow cove-lit dome, and yet the overall effect is sensual, not hard-edged. Stepped moldings, cubistic fireplaces, and built-in banquettes all act as scaling devices to balance the sweep of the public areas, while cove lighting and backlit stair treads enhance the magic at night.

The master bathrooms have retained their original Vitrolite panels, wrap-around mirrors, black marble basins, and floor controls for the faucets. The bedrooms are surprisingly small and one of them has been turned into a stylish home office. The tennis pavillion, like the living room, still allows you to imagine the year to be 1930. Approaching it across the lawn, it seems to be a simple cube, but the interior is a jewel-like composition of copper-framed linoleum panels and a stair balustrade of copper hoops. From the court, it resembles the proscenium arch of a theater, and you wait for the lights to come on and a screen to fill with the roaring lion of M-G-M.

Above, mirrored wall in the dining room.
Opposite, the dressing room.

One of the best-known and best-loved houses in America, Fallingwater, in Bear Run, Pennsylvania, may be Frank Lloyd Wright's masterpiece. It was commissioned by Edgar Kaufmann Sr., a Pittsburg department store tycoon who loved the arts and would, a decade later, invite Richard Neutra to do his best work in the design of a winter home in Palm Springs. The matchmaker and project supervisor for Fallingwater was Edgar Kaufmann Jr., who had apprenticed to Wright in Taliesin and would later become the impresario of design at the Museum of Modern Art in New York. In 1935, Wright's career was in eclipse and this job was a life-saver. And yet legend has it that he prepared nothing in advance of his first meeting with the client, but began sketching only when Kaufmann was already on his way, producing bold conceptual sketches with a flourish as he arrived.

Fallingwater is set in an idyllic forested estate in the Appalachians. It is a ninety-minute drive from Pittsburg, which was then the most polluted city in the world, its air heavy with the fumes of its steel plants. The contrast could not have been greater, and Wright exploited the natural beauty of the site by building a structural core that hugs the steep slope and cantilevering the living room and its terrace over a waterfall. From the house you can hear but not see the water, though steps lead down to its edge. The core is clad in fieldstone that seems to grow out of the natural rock; the decks and flat roof terraces are of smooth concrete, set off by steel windows in Wright's signature color, Cherokee red. You approach through the forest and suddenly it is there, perfectly composed, as thrilling on the tenth visit as the first.

Into this house Wright poured the pent-up ideas and energies of a decade of enforced idleness. The rock floors flow out through windows that open at the corners. There's a constant shift of levels and ceiling heights as you progress from the spacious living room to the snug bedrooms and the upper-level guest wing. Every turn brings a fresh view, out to the forest and in to a perfectly detailed yet rustic interior. Kaufmann's son, who spent a lot of time here before his death in 1989 and arranged for the transfer of ownership to a non-profit conservancy, recalls the social life of the early years. "One Christmas season we welcomed a ten-day continual flow of visitors," he recalled. "Marcel Breuer, the Moholy-Nagys, the Alfred Barrs, and other drifted in, were merry, and departed in deep snow. About half an hour after the Moholys drove off, the butler came in to announce, 'Mr. Mahogany is stuck in a ditch!'"

Every architect came to admire the house—though Philip Johnson complained that the sound of the water excited his bladder! Now, in the seventh decade of the house, the conservancy is undertaking a major restoration to stabilize a structure that far outdistanced the technology of the day. When complete it will allow a growing number of visitors to appreciate anew the genius of an architect who depended all his life on enlightened patrons like the Kaufmanns.

Most modern architects struggled to design standardized, afford-able housing based on a prototype that could be replicated, and nearly all were defeated by the innate conservatism of the con-struction industry and unions, loan officers and realtors. Frank Lloyd Wright, who is best known for creating one-of-a-kind residences for exceptional, often rich clients, also challenged the Bauhaus approach with his Usonian houses, and succeeded in building fifty-eight of them. "Usonia" was his acronym for the "United States of North America." He planned two ideal commu-nities of affordable wood and brick houses, which would employ similar features but be customized to the client and the site. The communities remained an idea on paper, but Usonian houses were built all over America.

The Herbert Jacobs House, in Madison, Wisconsin, built in 1936, was the prototype for the Usonian house. Its *L* plan defines two sides of the site and partly encloses the garden. The taller wing is for living, the lower for sleeping; plumbing is concentrated into a service core, and an open carport extends from the junction of the two wings. The Great Depression spurred fresh thinking in the American heartland, and the Jacobs house is astonishingly commodious for its size and cost ($5,000, plus a ten percent fee for Wright, who made frequent visits to the site from nearby Taliesin). The formal parlor gives way to an all-purpose living-dining room with built-in bookshelves and seating, and a window wall with French doors opening onto the garden. As the architect explained, "We did a great deal in the open plan when we took the hostess out of the kitchen . . . and made her a feature of her establishment."

Brick walls support the wide, shallow-pitched roof. Screen walls of battened boards with an insulated core were slotted in and stiffened by the addition of bookshelves and cabinets, or by turning the corners. The concrete floor is painted Cherokee red, adding warmth to the exposed wood and brick. Abundant natural light from the window walls is balanced by the narrow openings beneath the eaves on the outer sides. Over the past twenty years, a new owner has restored what had become derelict, using new materials like a rubber roof membrane within the structure but staying true to the surfaces and furnishings that Wright intended.

Above, the entry from the street.

The Gropius House, in Lincoln, Massachusetts, was built between 1937 and 1938. This landmark of modernism has a most unlikely location: a New England village, just a few minutes' walk from Walden Pond, and a short gallop from Concord, cradle of the American Revolution. Walter Gropius was also a revolutionary, a practitioner and teacher who founded the Bauhaus in 1919, fled Hitler's Germany to a teach at Harvard in 1937, and shaped the thinking of a whole generation of architects. As a new immigrant, he wanted to settle down with his wife and daughter in a house that was conveniently close to his office in Cambridge. It would be furnished with the sleek furniture he had retrieved from his apartment in Berlin, but outwardly it had to fit in with the neighbors' homes.

Gropius succeeded so well that it is hard now to imagine how startling this house must have seemed when it was new. The plain geometry, straight roofline, and ribbon windows recall the houses that Gropius and Marcel Breuer had designed for the Bauhaus masters in Dessau, Germany, twelve years before. The taut skin of vertical clapboards rising from a fieldstone base, the screen porch, and the fences that extend from either side—as well as the central stair hall with rooms opening off on two levels—are features that the architect admired in New England farmhouses.

A local landowner gave Gropius the plot of land and loaned him the money to build because, though she was an old, traditionally minded lady, she felt that everyone should be able to express themselves as they wanted. Though Gropius had always found himself in city apartments, he loved the countryside and lived happily here for the rest of his life. His widow, Ise, donated the house to the Society for the Preservation of New England Antiquities, which assumed responsibility after her death in 1983 and undertook a major restoration before opening it to the public.

Visitors can enjoy the property on two levels at once: as a daring experiment, crammed with fresh ideas and novel artifacts, and as an enduring part of the New England heritage. Early settlers adapted European models to the local climate and building materials; Gropius did the same, rooting modernism in this stony soil, and impressing skeptical neighbors by riding out the great hurricane of 1938. The clean lines and functional furnishings are enlivened with personal touches, from the sinuous hand-welded steel stair rail to the glass wall between bedroom and dressing area that allowed the owners to sleep with open windows while conserving heat in the rest of the house. Gropius's daughter, Ati, who grew up here and now keeps a watchful eye on the legacy, loved the fact that her bedroom opened onto a roof deck and an outside spiral stair that allowed her to come and go as she pleased. In this frugal, compact, energy-efficient house, Gropius showed Americans how they might live simply and in close touch with nature—as Thoreau had, for his contemporaries, almost a century before.

Kennth Frampton, in *American Masterworks*, wrote:

More sculptural than most photographs suggest, the Gropius House is a dynamic spatial composition that draws one toward the front door, through the passage of an over-sailing canopy and past an equally compelling wall plane executed in glass block. The warmth of this house, reinforced by the cork-tile flooring that runs throughout, distances this work from the more machinist functionalism of Gropius' Weimar designs. A sense of relaxed comfort pervades the interior, despite the freestanding glass-block wall that divides the study from the dining space and the Bauhaus furniture, designed by Marcel Breuer.

These Bauhaus elements, which Gropius shipped over during his exodus, are among the dwelling's prominent period pieces. Along with paintings by Laszlo Moholy-Nagy and Alexander Schawsinsky, they bestow a uniquely transatlantic aura; one that recalls the pioneering days of the Museum of Modern Art and Black Mountain College in North Carolina. This house evokes those halcyon years at Harvard when Joseph Hudnut charged Gropius and other emigre luminaries with the task of totally recasting the curriculum of the Graduate School of Design.

Not without irony, the Gropius House has now become the property of the Society for the Preservation of New England Antiquities. On the occasion of its fiftieth anniversary in 1988, the society restored the house and opened it to the public. In bequeathing it to the society Ise Gropius intended not only that the house should serve as an example of Gropius' contribution to modern architecture but also that its entire contents should provide a reminder of a way of life that was already becoming remote. To this end Walter Gropius' spectacles lie on top of his sketch pad and Ise's red evening dress hangs in the dressing room closet, mute reminders of another time.

On the second-floor deck, the opening on the right leads to an exterior spiral stairway.

Postwar Modernism

The Farnsworth House, in Plano, Illinois, was built between 1946 and 1951. This legendary house has an other-worldly perfection: It is an ethereal steel and glass pavilion that seems to float above an emerald meadow, framed by delicate trees and the soft eddy of the Fox River. That is not at all how its first owner, Chicago physician Dr. Edith Farnsworth experienced it. For her it was a nightmare. Construction stretched out, costs ran over the original estimates, and the architect, Ludwig Mies van der Rohe, sternly forbade her to install screens on the windows to keep the swarms of mosquitoes at bay. She went ahead and did so, but she froze in winter and sweltered in summer, sued the architect, and eventually moved to Italy.

A white knight in the person of Peter Palumbo, an English lord who had dreamed of this house since he was a schoolboy, rode to the rescue. He was visiting Chicago to discuss the office tower he had commissioned from Mies for a prominent site in London's financial district, heard the house was for sale, and drove out to see it. For him, it was love at first sight. He bought and restored the house to pristine condition, and opened it to the public. He used it himself for occasional visits to Chicago, installing contemporary artworks in the relandscaped gardens. Then disaster struck. In 1996 the river rose ten feet above its banks in a freak flood. A wall of muddy water and debris smashed through the plate glass windows, destroying furniture and the Primavera cabinets that divided the kitchen from the living room. Mies had died, but his grandson, Dirk Lohan, worked with Palumbo to restore the house once again. Recently, the long-suffering owner put the house up for sale and now another individual or institution will confront the challenge of maintaining it.

291

It would be easy to judge this house a white elephant, beautiful but uninhabitable, and sited in the path of danger. In many ways it is like a Bugatti, thrilling to race, and an object of envy to all who see it, but decidedly impractical for collecting groceries or ferrying kids to soccer practice. This is a house that shrugs off everyday concerns but allows the spirits to soar. Sitting alone in a Mies chair, watching the light gleam off the travertine paving, or strolling the grounds and coming upon this apparition at a turn in the path, is to experience a magical moment that is worth any price and every inconvenience. The house has survived a half-century and is so rigorously constructed that, properly maintained, it could last for centuries more.

The Glass House, in New Canaan, Connecticut, was built in 1949. When Frank Lloyd Wright came to see Philip Johnson in his newly completed Glass House, he stepped inside, looked around, and asked mockingly: "Am I indoors or am I out? Do I leave my hat on or do I take it off?" The host was delighted. The spirit of creative play is alive in this house, and in the dozen other structures that have joined it on a forty-acre estate that was once a farm and retains its drystone walls.

A Gatefold of Doorways and Windows of the Twentieth Century

Opposite, right
The massive concrete doors of the Hollyhock house in Los Angeles, California.

Overleaf
The Greenberg house in Los Angeles, California.

Johnson is the chameleon of twentieth-century architecture. He launched his career as a fervent advocate of modernism, practiced what he preached for two decades, and then switched allegiance to a dizzying succession of styles. The Glass House belongs to the period in which he venerated Mies, collaborated with him on the design of the Seagram Building in New York, but found ways of distinguishing his own work from that of the master. The Farnsworth house evokes a Greek temple in its purity and other-worldliness, the last in a succession of ideal villas that were sketched from the early 1920s on, and previously incarnated as the German Pavilion in Barcelona and the Tughendat house in Brno, Czechoslovakia. The Glass House, by contrast, seems low-key and down-to-earth—it was Johnson's first major building.

Left
The façade of the Susan Lawrence Dana house (see pages 230–235). The low walls of gray Roman brick, set off by buff cornice lines, serve as a foil for the bronze green plaster. The façade is also animated by the eaves, which tip up at the corners—a feature that Wright borrowed from the traditional Japanese house he visited at the World's Columbian Exposition of 1893 in Chicago.

Above
The John Storer house in Hollywood was one of five concrete-block homes Frank Lloyd Wright built in southern California. This is a view of the concrete-walled living room looking towards the balcony. Wright said, "Concrete is a plastic material—susceptible to the impress of imagination." Wright designed a block that could be molded on site into different patterns and could be easily handled by one person.

Above

The street façade of the F. C. Bogk house in Milwaukee by Frank Lloyd Wright. The fenestration shows the mastery of the architect's use of proportion, allowing the occupants privacy while bringing in long shafts of light through the simple stained glass patterns.

Right

The outside walls of the Glessner House, Chicago, (see pages 208–209) were built of rock-faced granite laid in horizontal courses of varying width. The lintels over the windows were flat but a large arch was used over the front door and a second arch over the side entrance porch.

Opposite, left
The entrance to the
Dolores del Rio
house in Santa Monica,
California.

Overleaf
This magnificent old
adobe house in northern
New Mexico is an excellent
example of a traditional
adobe structure updated by
allowing more exterior light
to come in. Many modern
adobe builders use skylights
in the same way that friars
in the Colonial period used
clerestory openings to bathe
their altars with natural
light. And the adaptable,
pliable, benefits of adobe
allows a 19th century
recycled conventional front
door to be fitted into a wall.

"I was building an American house," Johnson explained on building the
Glass House. "I like to get outdoors quickly, so I raised it only two steps
above the ground. It's anchored by a brick podium and a brick cylinder
that penetrates the roof. Mies didn't like that. His philosophy was based
on uninterrupted floating planes." The cylindrical brick bathroom and
fireplace was . . . inspired by a wartime memory of a wooden village
that had burned, leaving only the masonry elements standing. "Over my
chimney I slipped a steel cage with a glass skin," he says.

There is a pleasing informality about the way you enter through a
sliding glass door—often followed by dry leaves that blow in and settle
on the herringbone brick floor. Mies furniture is placed in sculptural
groupings to define the dining and sitting areas; the bed is concealed by
an armoire. "It's often written about as a house you cannot live in," says
Johnson. "I don't know why—I've been going there for nearly forty-five
years. Over the last ten years I've spent almost every weekend there, in
all seasons; in fog, snow, and moonlight. It gets a little cold in winter,
and warm in summer—but the doors give cross ventilation. You adapt."

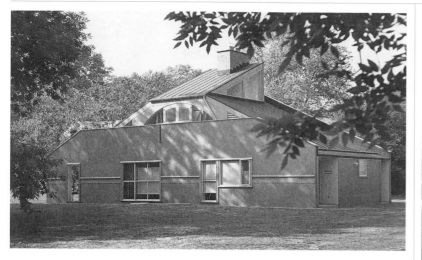

Built for his mother from 1961 to 1964, the Vanna Venturi House in Chestnut Hill, Philadelphia, Pennsylvania, represents postmodern architect Robert Venturi's first important project. Deceptively simple from the exterior, the Venturi House employs Classical architectural ideas in its substance and in its plan. Yet a quick look at its windows, which are located asymmetrically in multiple shapes and sizes around the house, betrays an unconventional and definitely non-Classical interior.

The front and back elevations of the house, as in Classical tradition, are symmetrical. Based on the pavilion at the rear of Palladio's Villa Maser, the front elevation acts as a Classical pediment. The split gable in the front elevation, unusual in 1964, reveals the central chimney block. Venturi wanted the house's design to serve as a symbolic device, thus the chimney, or hearth, was built so that it is the focal center of the house. The complexity of the interior spaces is also inferred by the off-center placement of the chimney in the chimney block.

A Classical dado, composed of wood molding, is unusual in that its placement is slightly higher than traditional. The dado is surrounded on the front façade with an arch that is composed of the same wood moulding. The unusual height of the dado and the arch projects the contradicting nature of what Robert Venturi was trying to attain with this house: "This building is complex and simple, open and closed, big and little. Inside and out, it is a little house that uses big scale to counterbalance the complexity. Complexity in combination with small scale in small buildings creates a nervous 'busyness,' whereas big scale in this small building achieves an appropriate architectural tension."

The interior spaces of the house show how truly complex the arrangement is despite the house's seemingly simple exterior. Though the overall plan for the house is symmetrical, this symmetry is broken up to make room for the center of the house—the fireplace-chimney—and for the staircase that wraps around the hearth. The fireplace and the chimney are angled distortedly and reflect the base of the staircase. Meanwhile, to wrap around the hearth, the width of the staircase changes, as does the general path of the stairs that lead to the upper floor.

What may also seem a surprise upon viewing the interior of the house are the furnishings within it. Venturi designed the house not so that it would contain modern furnishings, as was typical then of modern and postmodern buildings, but rather so that his mother could house the furniture she had collected over the years. This included a wide assortment of antiques plus other comfortable furnishings, such as the plush couch that resides in the living room.

Despite its interior complexities, Venturi designed a house for his mother that remains basic. As he has remarked, "Some have said my Mother's house looks like a child's drawing of a house—representing the fundamental elements of shelter—gable roof, chimney, door, and windows. I like to think this is so, that it achieves another essence, that of the genre that is house and is elemental."

Above, the studio/guest house.

At the far eastern tip of Long Island, where the names of Colonial British settlements alternate with those of the native Montauk tribe, new money has seeded old farms with elaborate summer houses, some ostentatiously over-scaled. The firm of Gwathmey Siegel has contributed its share of impressive beachfront palazzi for the super-rich. The Gwathmey House and Studio, in Amangassett, New York, built between 1965 and 1967, however, is a modest solo effort, Gwathmey's third project after graduating from Yale. It was designed for his parents and won immediate fame, establishing his reputation and launching a hugely successful career. The crisp platonic forms of the house are echoed in his father's painting studio/guest house across the lawn, and the twin structures circle each other gracefully, inviting comparison and focusing attention on their similarities and differences.

Both structures are clad, inside and out, in tightly fitted tongue-and groove cedar siding which has weathered to a soft gray. Rounded staircases and wedge-shaped lanterns push out from boxes that seem to have been cut out with an Exacto knife to reveal and shade expansive windows. To maximize views over the flat landscape, the double-height living-dining areas are located on the second floor of the house, with a mezzanine-level master bedroom above, guest bedrooms and the garage below. The second-floor studio has an exterior staircase and a guest suite tucked in underneath.

This house is the seed from which the later, grander houses flowered. It fuses the purist geometry of Le Corbusier with the rural vernacular. Natural wood softens the boxy forms and sharp edges, and marries the house to the pastoral landscape. The simplicity of the frame is enriched by felicitous details, such as the slender white brick chimney that is set at an angle to the plan, the redwood decking and birchwood cabinetry complementing the cedar, and the diversity and placement of the window openings.

The Douglas House, in Harbor Springs, Michigan, was built from 1971 to 1973. This was Richard Meier's tenth house, completed in his tenth year of practice. Until he saw an exhibition of Le Corbusier's work at New York's Museum of Modern Art, he had considered a career as an artist and was sharing a studio with Frank Stella. His earliest houses have a superficial resemblance to those of Charles Gwathmey: cut-away boxes of wood siding or brick that differ from Gwathmey's chiefly in their whiteness. This house is something else: an unabashed homage to the French master and the early moderns' fascination with transportation. It anticipates the Atheneum at New Harmony, Indiana, an institutional building that is even more nautical. The Douglas house, built for a couple from Grand Rapids, evokes the stacked decks of an ocean liner, set off by pipe railings, exterior metal stairs, rounded balcony, and twin funnels. An instant icon, it stands out boldly from a forest that drops away sharply to the sandy shore of Lake Michigan.

The Douglases were inspired by Meier's Smith house in Darien, Connecticut, and requested something similar for a site in a planned community. The architect made some preliminary drawings and showed them to the community's design watchdog who rejected them on the grounds that the windows were too large, the roof too flat, and the walls too white to fit in with the timid retro styling of the neighboring properties. The clients refused to be intimidated, sold their plot, and bought this far more exciting site, where there were no constraints on creativity.

The house has four levels and is set forward of the slope. It is entered at the top across a drawbridge that spans the void between the hillside and the rear façade; a lower bridge leads out into the garden. This immediately establishes the contrast between private

and public realms, as expressed by the solid wall to the rear and the glass that is wrapped around the other three sides, bathing the interior in light. In defiance of convention, the fireplace that would usually be set back as a focus for the interior is here a part of the façade, so that the flames are framed by the sky. As a later owner, J. Paul Beitler, observed: "Usually when people enter a house, they expect the outside to be brought in. In this house, the opposite occurs: you are transported outside and into the trees." And he praises "the sense of discipline carried through in each room down to the details. The impression of order and serenity reaches one on both a conscious and a subliminal level; when coming into the house, one has an immediate feeling of peace."

Born in Estonia, Louis Kahn worked for many years in obscurity before emerging as a tragic hero of architecture. He labored to create a few scattered masterpieces, but died, poor and unrecognized, of a heart attack in New York's Pennsylvania Station. The Salk Institute, the Kimbell Art Museum, and a dozen more of his buildings have a monumentality unmatched in our times. Kahn looked to the ancient world for inspiration, stubbornly refusing to compromise his principles and leaving many projects unrealized. His few houses are mostly located in or near Philadelphia. The Korman House, in Fort Washington, Pennsylvania, was built between 1971 and 1973, for a young developer, his wife and four sons in a suburb of that city, and was Kahn's last.

The rough-hewn grandeur and temple-like proportions of a Kahn house are unmistakable; you feel the owners should get into the spirit of the place by donning togas. However, the architect uses vertical cedar siding inside and out, and brick for the free-standing chimneys at either end, which tames the magnificence and makes the house an integral part of the seventy-acre estate. The ample scale brings a deep sense of serenity, notably in the double-height living room with its boldly articulated window wall framing the fields and the sky.

A massive fir staircase leads out of a lofty hall to the upstairs bedroom; another, at the center of the house, links the master suite to the den. The massive posts and one-inch planks recall, not Meier's liners, but a ship in the age of sail.

House VI, in West Cornwall, Connecticut, was built between 1972 and 1975. Richard Frank, a photographer, and his wife commissioned this 2,000-square-foot weekend house for a site in the rural northwest of a state that is often misperceived as a string of commuter towns leading to New York. As the name suggests, it was one in a series of experiments in three-dimensional geometry that began with House I in 1967. Peter Eisenman describes it as "a sensuous and playful environment, full of continuously changing light, shadows, color, and textures. The house is a studio landscape, providing an abstract background for the photography

of still life and people. In doing so, the house and its occupants become part of a series of daily 'living portraits.'"

In the late 1960s, at the beginning of his career, Eisenman was a member of a group that critics dubbed the " New York Five," along with Gwathmey, Meier, Michael Graves, and the late John Hedjuk. They were also known as the "Whites" for the chaste purity of their architecture, but their communality was short lived, and they have since moved in radically different directions. For a long time, Eisenman was thought to be too preoccupied with grids and the vaporings of French philosophers ever to create

habitable buildings. An early house in which the grid mandated a slot that sliced through the owners' double bed reinforced this prejudice.

Most bad boys eventually grow up and Eisenman, though still maddeningly arcane in utterance, has created a substantial body of work (notably the Wexner Center for the Visual Arts on the Columbus campus of Ohio State). His buildings challenge their users to make them fulfill useful purposes—but art and formal concerns still take precedence over utility, as they do here. It is perhaps best to regard House VI as minimal sculpture in the spirit of Sol LeWitt, and as a variation on the interlocking planes and spaces of Gerrit Rietveld's Schroeder House of 1924 in Utrecht. Like Philip Johnson, Eisenman is a formalist with no interest in the social (let alone socialist) agenda of creating model dwellings. At least House VI was inexpensive, being constructed from painted wood panels, and provides basic shelter for an agile couple willing to skip up narrow stairs and shoehorn themselves into the few furnished spaces.

323

The Graves House, in Princeton, New Jersey, was built between 1977 and 1993. In contrast to the cerebral diagrams of Eisenman, Michael Graves' work has a cartoonish charm that is best exemplified in his Disney hotels and the chubby Deco-ish housewares he designed for Target stores. An erudite talent run wild, he led the charge to postmodernism and remains loyal to that short-lived fashion, which is now the preferred costumery for suburban malls. Nobody is more adept than Graves in paraphrasing the past; he has scattered multicolored columns and pediments like confetti over a succession of large commercial buildings.

Graves' own house, an outwardly plain converted warehouse on the edge of the university town where he teaches and practices, is far more interesting. The *L*-plan storage facility was put up in 1926 by Italian masons who were building Princeton's Gothic dorms, and had fallen into disrepair when Graves bought it in 1970. He did a quick fix, moved in, and waited until he had the resources to do an ambitious remodel, which extended over fifteen years. This began with a new rendering of purplish-beige stucco which unifies the public and private wings, built of brick and of hollow tile.

Within, Graves has paid homage to Sir John Soane, the early-nineteenth-century British architect who spent his last years transforming a trio of London row houses into a magical domain that is half folly, half museum, and wholly entrancing. Graves has borrowed Soane's neo-classical linearity, tricks of perspective and trompe l'oeil effects. He employs shallow domes and barrel vaults, as well as fat and anorexic Tuscan columns of his own invention, to define a sequence of salons. The natural lighting and artificial illumination are brilliantly manipulated to model the spaces and enhance the drama of the interior as you move through it. Moldings and warm-toned stucco set off the Biedermeier furniture, a collection of Graves' own designs, classic architectural drawings, and fragments from antiquity.

The New South and West

The Spear House, in Miami, was built in 1978. Few houses have received such immediate and widespread recognition as this water-front residence; it achieved stardom on the television series *Miami Vice* and splashy coverage in fashion spreads, and was the site of colorful extravaganzas by the local firm of Arquitectonica. Five architects launched the firm in 1977, and its work expressed the spirit of the city at that time: fast-paced, colorful, corrupt, and infused with the energy of newly arrived latinos. This was the job that catapulted Arquitectonica to fame—an exotic home in the retro community of Miami Shores on Biscayne Bay. It was built for the father of partner Laurinda Hope Spear, who designed it with her husband and partner Bernardo Fort-Brescia.

In contrast to the debased deco of the neighboring houses, this residence is an abstraction of the concept of shelter, comprising a series of layered indoor-outdoor spaces. Black olives screen the façade of pink stucco and glass block. A short alleé of royal palms defines the approach, but the entry is set to one side, up a flight of red steps. A porthole frames the raised pool where Dr. Spear, a thoracic surgeon, did his laps, and reflections from the water sparkle off the glass block. Beyond is a canopy-shaded terrace and a master suite that looks out to the front garden. Within the house is a double-height corridor, with steps at either end leading up to bedrooms overlooking the bay. The lofty living room has a floor-to-ceiling grid of casement windows that capture, mosaic-like, a panorama of water and sky with a distant view of the far coastline. The interiors are painted a pale blue-gray that captures the shifts of the light that filters through the layers of the house.

"Geological architecture" is how Stanley Saitowitz describes the relationship of his houses to the land, and that term aptly describes The DiNapoli House, in Los Gatos, California, built between 1987 and 1990, which he designed for Philip and Jennifer DiNapoli in the hills between San Jose and Santa Cruz. The plan is evident as you approach from above, looking out over the stone-faced house on its promontory and an eleven-acre wooded estate. Two wings bracket the open space of the promontory, tracking the contours, and remaking the ground as their roofs. One contains the dining area and guest rooms, the other incorporates the master suite, library, and gym. Between is the lofty living room, a steel-framed pavilion with a projecting roof deck that separates the entry court from the garden court.

Saitowitz, who began creating earth-hugging shelters in his native South Africa before reestablishing his practice in San Francisco, was inspired by the terraced ruins of Machu Pichu and the vernacular-inspired houses of Luis Barragan in Mexico. A visit to the Barcelona Pavilion reminded him of Mies' early projects for country houses in which planar brick walls would seem to slide across the site, defining spaces to either side. That concept has been amplified here, where the walls have become the wings that define and enclose space, and support terraces that step down the slope. These provide a fifth elevation that can be enjoyed from a barn at the top of the site which doubles as an office and as a garage for a vintage car collection.

From the point of entry, stone steps and terraces create a kind of amphitheater within a living room that serves as a place to entertain large numbers of guests. The steps and the exposed structural beams and columns give the huge volume a human scale. Light filters in from high-level windows, and a gallery leads out to the roof terraces of the wings to either side. In contrast to the rough-textured wood and stone of this principal room, creamy marble dominates the master suite. Here, and throughout the house, there is a feeling of serenity and openness.

The Greenberg House, in Los Angeles, was built in 1991. Audrey and Arthur Greenberg had lived for twenty-five years on this leafy site in the Brentwood district of Los Angeles in a Mexican-style house that was, like its eclectic neighbors, a pale copy of an exhausted genre. As patrons of contemporary art and music they deserved something more appropriate to the times and the place. They turned to the heir of Luis Barragan, the Mexican architect Ricardo Legorreta, and he created a house that expresses the essential spirit of his country. Like Adolf Loos, who stripped surface ornament to reveal the innate beauty of mass, space, and materials, so did Barragan—and now Legoretta—purge Colonial excess and find inspiration in the impassive walls and searing colors of their native vernacular.

Legorreta has written eloquently of how the wall opens, allows glimpses of secret gardens, or conceals what lies beyond: "Tragedy, strength, joy, romance, peace, light, and color, all of these qualities are in Mexican walls."

This is a house of mystery and stillness that unfolds in an ordered sequence of blank and pierced walls, dark and luminous spaces. The theme is boldly stated in the walled forecourt, where yuccas and a group of towering palms rise from an expanse of river-washed pebbles. Two towers, one rotated at a forty-five-degree angle, bracket walls of hand-troweled, rough-textured stucco in shades of sand, mustard, and bright yellow. Grille-like slits are lined with purple; magenta and cerise enrich other reveals. You are reminded that southern California is desert country that would revert to nature without continued irrigation, and these walls respond to the brilliance of the sun, capturing the chiaroscuro of light and shade and shielding the interiors from its heat. Most modern architects in this region take their cue from a climate that allows outdoor living year-round, and create lightweight shelters that open up on every side; Legorretta is inspired by an older tradition of dramatizing the contrast between exterior and interior.

There is a sense of progression as you move inside from the small entry court. The living areas flow out of atria and passages with glimpses of interior courts. In some of these spaces, the color is so intense that you feel you are walking into an abstract light painting, like those of Dan Flavin. Glass is set directly into the stucco and is placed to frame views of the garden, which was landscaped by Mia Lehrer and Scott Sebastian. Floors are wood strip or are covered with Mexican tiles or the limestone that is also used on the terrace. One tower contains the master bedroom—Arthur Greenberg delighted the architect by telling him he had never slept better than here—with a media room above; the other has a dining room below an office. Steps lead down to the garden and the pool, and your appreciation of the grass, trees, and water is intensified by your passage through the house.

343

The Empié House, in Carefree, Arizona. was built in 1986. Living simply in a natural paradise has been a recurring fantasy of city-dwellers, who imagine themselves as Thoreau in his hut beside Walden Pond, as pioneers on the prairie, or even as primitive cave dwellers, hunting and gathering. "They've paved over paradise/Put up a parking lot," as Joni Mitchell sang, but the dream endures, and a lucky few live it out. Bill and Sunny Empie found their ideal, ten-acre site amid massive granite boulders in the aptly named community of Carefree—an environmentally responsive refuge for exiles from the air-conditioned nightmare of Scottsdale, Arizona, with its malls and megamansions. They turned to Santa Fe architect Charles Foreman Johnson to create a house that would be as at home in this awesome setting as a lizard on a rock.

Like a lizard, this Pueblo-style house slips and slides among the boulders, peeking out and darting within the crevices, inhabiting the spaces that are enclosed by the stones and were earlier the home of Hohokam people. Pottery fragments from those first residents are displayed on shelves alongside the owners' collection of Native American crafts. Vigas project from a rotunda that evokes a tribal kiva. Light filters in through glass-filled fissures between the rocks or from above, gleaming off polished, integrally colored concrete floors. Reinforced concrete block, molded to resemble adobe, bonds to the granite, defines rooms and a hearth, and leads you forward from one rounded enclosure to the next. As Johnson noted, "the challenge was to find the house plan in the boulders."

Subtly he improved on Nature, widening an existing opening, and tempering the climatic extremes of the desert. But nothing is done to tame or encroach upon the physicality and tactility of the boulders. You brush against them or duck under them, constantly aware of their timeless power. In its tight enclosure and labyrinthine complexity, this house intensifies your appreciation of the vast emptiness beyond. It sits lightly on the land, respecting the flow of space and the scale of the rock formations. Johnson has done well by doing less.

When architects build for themselves they enjoy unlimited freedom of expression but have to live with, and be judged by, the product of their creativity. Steven Haas is a modernist at heart but he wanted to respect the traditional forms and materials of the neighboring farm buildings in the Berkshires on the western edge of Massachusetts. The Haas House, in Alford, Massachusetts, was built in 1992 and 1993. Taking as his model the post-and-beam wooden barn, he designed a simple gable-roofed rectangle, fifty-eight feet wide and seventy feet long. The house is supported by exposed posts and beams of steel over glass window walls that wrap around its three sides. These walls are stepped back on the east and west sides in a symmetrical pattern to create a series of covered, slate-paved terraces. The house is located on a knoll at the northern end of a valley and Haas has taken the long grasses right up to the transparent north and south sides to give the illusion that they are flowing through the glass. The same effect is repeated in the detached carport, which mimics the structure of the house.

A glass prow emerges from the west gable to direct attention from the master bedroom and the office above towards a stream set amid trees. The east façade is recessed to form a covered porch, leading into a living room that opens up to the gable. The living room is lit from a big window over the porch and a skylight that casts two squares of sunlight around the room. Once a year, these exactly fill the bluestone coffee table, fabricated from a larger piece that was delivered to the site in a pallet containing stones for the walls. A granite lintel from a Maine farmhouse has been recycled as a mantel over the slate-sheathed fireplace. Windows and skylight can be opened to provide cross ventilation and to evacuate hot air. The covered terraces can be illuminated to maintain the transparency of the glass after nightfall.

The house has proved itself in every season, remaining snug when the snow is piled high all around, and staying cool and airy on the hottest summer day. Every season provides a different experience and the owners have seeded the long grass with wildflowers that provide a colorful carpet in the early spring. Haas jokes that he and his wife would pinch themselves in their first year of occupancy to be sure they weren't dreaming this idyll.

353

Urban Renewal

Almost a century ago, trade unions and church groups in Amsterdam hired progressive architects to design high-density working-class housing estates that were hailed for their humanity and have been cherished ever since. They are now acclaimed as landmarks of early modernism, pointing forward to the municipal developments that were erected all over the Netherlands, Germany, and Scandinavia in the 1920s. These sensitively scaled, richly landscaped communities also expressed the spirit of the times and have been maintained in pristine condition. In Britain and the United States, by contrast, the poor are often regarded as an underclass to be housed in shoddily built and poorly maintained barracks. Within a decade these "projects" have begun to fall apart and become crucibles of crime; many, starting with the Pruitt-Igoe towers in St. Louis, have been demolished.

In 1993, Congress approved a program called Hope VI to replace the most decrepit public housing with livable neighborhoods that draw on the ideas of the New Urbanism—a misleading label for a return to traditional town planning. In place of the low density, curvilinear labyrinth of suburbia, its advocates argue for a tight-knit grid of small blocks with houses that face onto through streets—a pattern that worked well for centuries and was foolishly abandoned by enthusiastic supporters of the Garden City Movement and then by every tract house builder.

At Park DuValle in Louisville, the Pittsburg firm of Urban Design Associates has created one of these new urban communities: a mixed-income development of 1,075 units that replaces a grim 1950s development on a ninety-five-acre site. The streets that were formally severed from surrounding neighborhoods to quarantine the residents have been opened up, and a parkway has been extended to improve access from the city. The houses are superficially similar; however, 450 are for sale, and the rest are multiple-unit rental properties. From a social viewpoint, the new development is a giant leap forward. Architecturally, the strategy is to make the units as retro as those in middle-class suburbs to remove the stigma from public housing. Urban Design Associates recently completed a similiar project in Charlotte, North Carolina, transforming a once troubled area into a mixed-income neighborhood, shown on the right.

In the United States, the concept of community seems inseparable from a collective wallow in misty-eyed nostalgia for ye olde—whether it's the affluent private settlement of Seaside, Disney's intensively regulated Celebration, or the typical spec suburb. In a democracy where everyone watches the same sitcoms and shares the same vision of the good life, homogenization may be inevitable. Sadly, low-income tenants don't have many choices and this may be the best they can hope for.

Glossary

abacus: In classical architecture, the flat slab topping a capital.

acanthus: Carving modeled after the serrated leaves of the acanthus plant, native to the Mediterranean region and used on Corinthian columns.

adobe: Unbaked clay brick, dried by the sun, introduced by the Spanish settlers for house-building in the southwestern United States.

applique ornament: Usually carved wood, fastened to a surface of a building.

apron: A horizontal cross member or framing element used below a chair seat, tabletop, or the understructure of a case piece; it is often shaped along the lower edge for decorative effect. It is also known as a skirt.

arcade: A line of arches supported by columns forming a roofed passageway.

arch: A curved structure made of wedge-shaped stones or bricks, spanning an opening and capable of bearing the weight of the material above it.

architrave: The shaped frame around a door or window opening; in classical architecture, the lowest member of an entablature.

ashlar: Square-edged blocks of stone, laid horizontally and joined vertically to form walls.

atrium: A light-filled hall or court located in the center of a building.

back splat: The central support of a chair back.

balloon frame: A simplified method of timber-frame construction, avoiding interior supports, that became popular in the United States during the late nineteenth and early twentieth centuries.

baluster: An upright, usually turned, vertical support of a stair rail, table, or chair; often with a vase-shaped outline.

balustrade: A handrail supported by a series of balusters or pillars.

bargeboard: A wide, flat board that seals the space below the roof, between the tiles and the wall, on a gable end. Bargeboards often have decorative carving or pierced decoration. It is also called a vergeboard.

Baroque: The bold architectural style of the late Renaissance that followed the unrestrained Mannerist style and is characterized by exuberant but organized decoration and composition.

barrel vault: A straight, continuous arched vault or ceiling in tunnel form, either semi-circular or semi-elliptical in profile.

battlement: A notched wall at the top of a medieval-styled building originally for the purpose of fortification.

Bauhaus: An art school founded in 1919 in Weimar, Germany, by Walter Gropius. Artists, and architects worked together designing functional forms for the ideal buildings of the future.

bay window: A projection with a window on a house façade. It may be curved (bow window) or angular in plan.

berm: An artificially created mound of soil or earth.

bonnet top: A broken-arch pediment backed by boards.

bracket foot: A support formed by two pieces of wood that join at the corner.

breakfront: Having a protruding central section.

bressumer: A large horizontal beam that spans a fireplace or other opening;

breezeway: A roofed passage open at the sides between separate buildings.

broken-arch pediment: A roughly triangular-shaped top patterned by opposing S-shaped arches that remain open at the apex; found on American tall-case furniture of the mid-eighteenth century.

broken pediment: A pediment in which one or both cornices are not continuous; a gap in the crown, sometimes filled with an urn or another motif.

bureau: A low desk or writing table with drawers.

cabriole leg: An S-shaped furniture leg on which the knee curves out and the ankle curves in, ending in an ornamental foot.

cantilever: A projecting beam that is supported at one end only. It usually supports a structure, like a balcony, where supports cannot be placed or are not desired.

capital: The top part of a column, usually decorated, and larger than the shaft of the column.

cartouche: A decorative scroll or shield-shaped ornamental panel.

caryatid: A supporting column in the form of a stylized female figure. Male figures were termed adantes.

cheval glass: A full-length mirror fitted on a four-legged frame with crossbars and flanking uprights, which allows it to tilt.

clapboard (pronounced "kla'berd"): A thin board that, when laid horizontally and overlapped, creates a weathertight outer wall surface on a timber-framed building.

classical: Having to do with the style of the ancient Greek or Roman periods.

claw-and-ball foot: A foot carved in the form of an animal or bird claw grasping a ball.

colonnade: A series of columns supporting arches.

column: A vertical member consisting of a nearly cylindrical shaft, with a base and capital used as a support or ornament in building.

Composite: A classical Order in architecture where columns combine Corinthian acanthus leaves with Ionic scrolls.

corbel: A projecting stone or timber block, supporting a horizontal member such as a beam.

Corinthian: The latest and most ornate of the classical Orders of architecture. The column is slender and usually fluted, the capital elaborately carved with acanthus leaves.

cornice: An ornamental crowning—typically molded; similar to the top of an entablature in architecture that projects along the top of a wall, pillar, side of a building, or a piece of case furniture.

crenelation: A pattern of square indentations, often called battlements.

cresting: An ornamental finish, usually of wood or metal, at the top of a building, such as the ridge of a roof.

crest rail: The top horizontal rail of a chair, settee, or sofa.

cyma curve: An S-shaped or double-curved line, one half of which is concave, the other half is convex.

cupola: A dome, usually small, topping a roof or turret, that lets light or air into a building.

dado: The lower wall surface, from the chair rail down to the skirting board.

demilune: Semicircular, or half-moon, in shape.

desk and bookcase: A tall case piece that includes an upper section fitted with shelves and partitions for books and papers, and a lower section that includes a writing surface, often with drawers or cabinet doors below. It is also known as a secretary-bookcase.

dished top: A tabletop, often hewn from a single board, that features a shallow raised rim.

dog-leg stair: Two flights of stairs parallel to each other with a half landing in between.

Doric: The earliest and plainest of the classical Orders. Doric columns usually have no base; the shaft is thick and broadly fluted, the capital spare and unornamented.

dormer: An upright window that projects from a sloping roof.

drop leaf: A hinged extension that is attached to the stationary top of a table so that it can be folded down when not in use.

easy chair: An upholstered armchair with a winged high back and enclosed padded arms. It is also known as a wing chair.

eaves: The lower edge of a roof that projects beyond the wall underneath.

entablature: The part of a classical building resting on the top of columns, made up of an architrave, frieze, and cornice.

elevation: The external face of a building.

escutcheon: The plate around a keyhole.

fall front: The hinged cover of a desk or secretary that folds out to form a writing surface.

fanlight: A semicircular window above a door, with glazing radiating out like a fan or sunburst. It is sometimes called a transom window.

fenestration: The arrangement of windows in a building.

finial: An ornament on top of a spire, roof, post, or canopy.

fireback: A decorated iron plate at the back of a fireplace that protects the wall and reflects heat.

Flemish bond: A form of brickwork in which, on each course, headers and stretchers alternate.

finial: A shaped ornament at the crest of a roof, or top of a tower, canopy, or a piece of case furniture.

figure: The grain pattern displayed on a cut piece of wood.

fluting: Decorative carving in the form of grooves derived from Classical columns.

fretwork: A form of openwork or low-relief carving that resembles a geometric grid pattern or latticework.

frieze: A flat or sculpted ornamental band on furniture; it runs horizontally, such as on the apron of a table or on the area beneath a pediment molding.

gesso: Plaster mixed with a binding material; it is used for relief work or as a ground for painting or gilding.

gilding: To coat with a thin layer of gold or a gold-colored paint.

gable: The triangular portion of the end wall of a building under a ridge roof.

geodesic: Having to do with a system of mathematics used to study curves, such as the curvature of the earth or dome structures.

gingerbread: Ornate wood decoration used in Victorian-style buildings.

girt: A horizontal supporting beam.

gable: That part of the wall immediately under the end of a pitched roof, cut into a triangular shape by the sloping sides of the roof.

gallery: A mezzanine supported over the primary interior space of a building; also, a long room used originally for outdoor exercise and later for the display of pictures.

gambrel roof: A roof with a double pitch, resembling a mansard roof.

girandole: A branched candleholder with a backplate fixed to a wall or overmantel.

half-landing: A landing halfway up a flight of stairs.

header: A brick laid so that only its short face is visible.

half-timber: A type of construction in which spaces formed by a timber frame are filled in with stone, bricks, or wattle and daub, the frame left exposed.

high chest: A tall two-part case piece consisting of an upper case with drawers that rests on top of a lower section, also with drawers, that is raised on legs.

highboy: A high chest.

joist: Intermediate parallel beams that support a floor or ceiling

incising: A carving technique in which a fine, sharp instrument is used to produce a lined pattern.

inlay: Ornamentation of Flemish origin that involves the skilfull insertion of patterned material (such as wood veneers) into the surface.

intaglio: Low-relief decorative carving.

inglenook: A recessed space beside a fireplace, usually housing a bench.

Ionic: One of the classical Orders of architecture, characterized by fluted columns and prominent volutes on the capitals.

keystone: The central stone in the curve of an arch or vault.

leaded lights: Small panes of glass set into cames (lead strips) to form a window.

lintel: A supporting wood or stone beam across the top of an opening such as that of a door or window.

loggia: A pillared gallery that is open on one side.

lopers: The decorative handholds that front the sliding support rails of a fall-front desk.

louver: One of a series of overlapping slats (for example, in window shutters).

lunette: A semicircular opening, as in a lunette window.

lustre glass: An iridescent glass, of the type made by Tiffany in the United States.

mansard roof: A roof with two slopes, the lower steeper to allow extra roof space for the attic rooms.

mantel: The frame surrounding a fireplace; often used to denote just the shelf (mantel shelf).

module: A prefabricated, standardized, interchangeable piece or part of a dwelling unit.

moulding: A decorative contour, in wood or stone.

mullion: An upright bar that vertically divides a window or other opening.

molding: A band of wood, either projecting or incised, that has been shaped by a molding plane.

mounts: All the decorative and functional metal hardware, including drawer pulls, escutcheons, and hinges, applied to furniture.

newel post: The post at the end of a staircase, usually attached to both the handrail and the string; on a circular staircase, the central post around which the stairs curve.

oculus: A circular opening in a wall or in the top of a dome.

Order: In classical architecture, a particular style of column and entablature, each with its own distinctive proportions and detailing. The Five Orders are Doric, Ionic, Corinthian, Tuscan, and Composite. The first three are derived from ancient Greek architecture; Tuscan and Composite are Roman adaptations of the earlier Greek models.

oriel: A bay window on an upper floor.

overmantel: A decorative treatment above a fireplace, often incorporating a painting or a mirror.

ogee curve: An S-shaped or reverse curve; similar to a cyma curve.

ormolu: Gilded bronze or brass made in imitation of gold and often used for furniture mounts.

outshot: A projection of, or an addition to, a building.

pad foot: A simple rounded or oval-shaped carved foot.

Palladian style: An interpretation of the classical style developed by Andrea Palladio (1508–80), the Italian architect.

palisade: A strong wooden fence.

parapet: A low wall placed to protect any spot where there is a sudden drop, for example, at the edge of a balcony or housetop.

patina: Surface texture and color acquired over time from general use and exposure.

pattern book: A book of designs for architectural details based on the revived principles of Classical architecture.

pedestal table: A table supported by a central column, commonly leading to a tripod base.

pediment: An ornamental triangular top across a portico, door, window, or piece of furniture; any similar triangular decorative piece over a doorway, fireplace or other feature. A pediment that is open on top is called a broken pediment.

pendant: An ornament hanging down from an arch, ceiling, or roof.

pent roof: A narrow roof sloping in one direction.

piazza: A broad veranda along one or more sides of a house.

piecrust table: A common term used to describe a circular tilt-top tea table or candle stand with a scalloped, molded edge. It was set on a single leg with three feet.

pier table: A side table, often placed in a dining room or parlor under a mirror, or between two windows (the architectural term for that wall space is pier).

pilaster: A flat rectangular column that projects in low relief from a wall or piece of furniture.

pitch: The angle or steepness of a roof.

plinth: A square block of the base of a column that serves as a base for a statue, vase, or finial.

porte-cochere: A porch wide enough to allow access for a carriage.

portico: A roofed entrance porch, usually with columns.

post-and-beam construction: A system of framing where heavy timber posts and beams are used.

purlin: Horizontal roof beams used to support roof rafters between the roof ridge and the eave.

quoin: A rectangle of stone, wood, or brick used in vertical series to decorate corners of buildings.

rafter: One of a series of parallel sloping roof members designed to support the roof. The rafters of a flat roof are often called joists.

rail: A horizontal framing member that extends from one vertical support to another, as in the crest of a chair.

rat-tail hinge: A hand-wrought door hinge featuring a heart-shaped terminal with a curled or winding tip that resembles a rat's tail.

reeding: Convex vertical carving. The reverse of fluting.

retaining wall: Any wall subjected to lateral pressure such as a bank of earth.

rebate or **rabbet:** a channel or groove cut into a surface edge (usually of wood) to receive another member.

rose-head nail: A hand-forged nail used in America during the seventeenth and eighteenth centuries; it has an irregularly shaped, slightly raised head that roughly resembles an open rose.

rustication: The rough finish given to projecting wood or stonework in a building made by deep chiselling. The edges or margins were left smooth.

sash window: A window formed with glazed wooden frames that slide up and down in grooves by means of counterbalanced weights. The standard form has two moveable sashes and is called a "double-hung sash."

sconce: a wall bracket for holding a light, particularly candles.

scroll: A decorative motif in the shape of the letter *S*.

scroll pediment: A trade term used to describe a broken-arch pediment.

secretary-bookcase: *See* **desk and bookcase**.

shingle: A thin piece of wood or other material, used to cover the roof and walls of a house. Shingles are laid in overlapping rows with the thicker ends showing.

shoe: A horizontal molded piece of wood attached to a chair's rail at the bottom of the back, into which the splat is fitted.

slip seat: A removable chair seat, made of cane, rush, or upholstery, that is designed to rest in the four seat rails of a chair.

soffit: The underside of a beam, arch, or other architectural element; also, the reveal of the head of a door or window.

spindle: A slender decorative turned piece of wood, similar to a baluster, often used on chair backs.

splat: The center support in back of a chair, often elegantly shaped and decorated

stepped gable: The gable end of a building that is constructed with a series of steps along the roof slope but independent of it.

stile: One of the two upright vertical side supports in a chair back that support the crest rail.

stretcher: A horizontal bracing member set between the legs of a chair, table, or the like for added strength and stability.

stringing: A narrow line of decorative inlay set into a contrasting primary wood on furniture.

stucco: A fine cement or plaster used on the surface of walls, moldings and other architectural ornaments. By the nineteenth century, stucco was generally used as a term for exterior rendering.

studs: The upright timbers in a timberframed building.

summer beam: A principal rafter or load-bearing beam, usually spanning the width of a room.

terracotta: unglazed, fired clay used for tiles, architectural ornament, garden pots, etc.

transom: the horizontal member across the top of a door, or across the top or middle of a window.

trompe l'oeil: a decorative effect, such as a painting of architectural detail or a vista, that gives the illusion of reality.

truss: A wooden framework in the shape of a bridge or large bracket, used to support timbers, such as those in a roof.

tie beam: A horizontal timber beam so situated that it ties the principal rafters of a roof together and prevents them from thrusting out of line.

tracery: A pattern of intersecting bars or a plate with leaflike decoration in the upper part of a Gothic window.

transom: A series of panes or lights above a door.

turret: A small tower often on the corner.

tilt-top table: A pedestal table fitted with a birdcage mechanism or block beneath the top that allows it to tilt when not in use.

toleware: A term of French derivation for paint-decorated tinware.

torchére: A tall stand with a very small top that is intended to hold a candlestick, lamp, or decorative object.

turnings: Furniture elements, such as balusters and spindles, that have been shaped on a lathe.

tympanum: The recessed front-facing board contained within the upper and lower cornices of a pediment.

veneer: A thin slice of wood used as a surface covering on a base, or less expensive, wood to give it a finished appearance.

vernacular: A term describing rural architecture, built to suit a peculiar locality, with little stylistic pretension.

veranda: A large porch along one or more sides of a house.

vestibule: A passage, hall, or chamber immediately between the outer door and the inside of a building.

viga: A beam that supports the roof in Indian and Spanish type dwellings.

volutes: In classical architecture, spiral scrolls, most characteristically forming the capital of a Greek Ionic column; scroll-shaped brackets.

wainscot: The simple, early form of wooden panelling, either full height or on the lower half of a wall.

wattle and daub: Interlaced sticks roughly plastered with a mixture of clay and chopped straw, sometimes reinforced with horsehair as a binding agent.

widow's walk: A rooftop platform or narrow walkway, often used as a lookout for ships on eighteenth- and nineteenth-century New England coastal houses.

Windsor chair: A chair designed with a multiple-spindle back that fits into a woodplank seat that is supported below by legs that splay outward.

wing chair: *See* **easy chair**.

Acknowledgments and Credits

We would like to thank the following for their help in the preparation of this book:
William Nathaniel Banks, Richard Bergmann, Sandra Bergmann, Corina Carusi, Steven Haas, Elaine Rocheleau, June Sprigg, Peggy Strong, and Brian Thompson.

The photographs are by Michael Freeman and Paul Rocheleau except for those on the pages 302–305 that were used by courtesy of Venturi, Scott Brown and Associates.

Michael Freeman:
Pages 2, 14, 15, 16, 17, 18, 19, 22, 23, 24, 25, 54, 55, 57, 62, 68, 72, 73, 75, 76, 77, 82, 83, 86–87, 118–119, 120–121, 138, 139, 152–153, 163, 215, 216–217, 218–219, 221, 222, 223, 224, 225, 236, 239, 244, 245, 246–247, 248–249, 250–251, 252–253, 254, 255, 262–263, 264–265, 266–267, 268–269, 334–335, 336–337, 338–339, 340–341, 342–343, 344–345, 346–347, 348–349, 350, 351

Paul Rocheleau:
Pages 4–5, 8–9, 20, 21, 26, 27, 28, 29, 30, 31, 32, 33, 34, 35, 36, 37, 38, 40, 41, 42, 43, 44, 45, 46, 47, 48, 49, 50, 51, 52, 53, 54, 55, 56, 58, 59, 60, 61, 62, 63, 64, 65, 66, 67, 68, 69, 70, 71, 72, 73, 74, 75, 77, 78, 79, 80–81, 82–83, 84, 85, 88, 89, 90, 91, 92, 93, 94, 95, 96, 97, 98, 99, 100, 101, 102, 103, 104, 105, 106–107, 108, 109, 111, 112, 113, 114, 115, 116–117, 122, 123, 124, 125, 126, 127, 128, 129, 130, 131, 132–133, 134–135, 136, 137, 140, 141, 142, 143, 144, 145, 146–147, 148, 149, 150, 151, 154, 155, 156, 157, 158, 159, 160, 161, 162, 164–165, 166, 167, 169, 170, 171, 172, 173, 174, 175, 176, 177, 178–179, 180–181, 182, 183, 185, 186, 187, 188, 189, 190, 191, 192, 193, 196, 197, 198, 199, 200, 201, 202, 203, 204, 205, 206, 207, 208, 209, 210, 211, 212, 213, 214, 215, 226, 227, 228, 229, 230, 231, 232–233, 234, 235, 256–257, 258–259, 260, 261, 271, 272–273, 274–275, 276–277, 278–279, 280, 281, 282–283, 284, 285, 286, 287, 288–289, 290, 291, 292, 293, 294–295, 296, 297, 298–299, 300, 301, 306, 307, 308, 310–311, 312, 313, 314, 315, 316, 317, 318, 319, 320–321, 322, 323, 324, 325, 326, 327, 328, 329, 330, 331, 332, 333, 352, 353, 354, 355